Emperor's Handbook
State Grade Society Doctrines

How to build and maintain influence in a modern media society.

Sami Leino

Copyright
© Emperor's Handbook: State Grade Society Doctrines
Sami Leino
All rights reserved 2016.
Edited by Megan McCullough.
FIRST EDITION

ISBN 978-952-71-4302-5 (Hardcover and paperback)
ISBN 978-952-71-4303-2 (PDF)
ISBN 978-952-71-4304-9 (EPUB)
ISBN 978-952-71-4305-6 (Kindle)
Cover, design, layout, content graphics are copyright of the author unless otherwise stated. All trademarks and business names are property of their respected owners. This book does not endorse any of the brands mentioned herein. Some of the internet links that were available at the time of writing may not be present in the future.
All rights reserved. No part of this publication may be reproduced, distributed, or transmitted in any form or by any means, including photocopying, recording, or other electronic or mechanical methods, without the prior written permission of the author, except in the case of brief quotations embodied in critical reviews and certain other noncommercial uses permitted by copyright law.

SAMI LEINO

Megan McCullough provided splendid editorial advisory. Unconditional strength was given by my wife Heidi and our dachshund Luigi.

Thank you.

"Anti-social behavior is a trait of

intelligence in a world full of conformists."

Nicola Tesla

..for Heidi, as always.

Index

Prologue 9

1. Who Believes in Western Saga? 15
    AILING AMERICA - TAILING EUROPE.................................... 15
    HYPERPOLARIZATION AND STAGNATION 35
    ENTERTAINMENT POLITICS... 39

2. Influence in Modern Media Age............................... 45
    THIS ISN'T A POPULARITY CONTEST, OR IS IT? 45
    PEAKED US POWER - PAST OR AHEAD? 49
    SYSTEM OF BELIEFS 55
    HUMAN PERCEPTION.. 57
    SOCIAL MASKS AND TRAIT OF SISU 63
    DEMOCRACY - AFFLUENCE AND INFLUENCE 67

3. The Good, The Bad, and The Ugly............................ 71
    MEDIA CRISIS RECOVERY 81
    TRAUMA OF AN IMAGE 90
    MEDIA BUILDING ON 9/11/2001 94

4. Smart Power.. 99
    NATION STATE BRAND... 99
    IMPLICATIONS OF POWER BUILD-UP 109
    ERODING AND DEGRADING POWER 111
    CHARM OF CHINA... 115

5. Society Doctrine 123
    FROM MEDIA DOCTRINES TO SOCIETY DOCTRINE 123
    PILLARS, SOURCES AND LEVELS OF POWER 127
    DEVELOPMENT OF POWER, 1850 - 2020 133

6. Media and Tactics.. 139
    MASS PERSUASION - METHODS AND TECHNIQUES 145
    TIME DECAY OF INFLUENCE 164

7. Superpowers in The Making................................... 175
    TERRORISM, PHASES AND MEDIA 175

RUSSIAN MEDIA-MACHINE 185
8. Conclusions... **195**
PROLIFERATED MEDIA CAPABILITIES............................... 195
End Words... **205**
Appendix... **209**
COLD WAR AND POPULAR CULTURE................................ 209
Sources **223**

Prologue

We're sailing in unchartered waters, in an archipelago of perils, a new era, that started after the West lagged in economic growth for a decade; after Russia invaded Crimea, millions of emigrants flowed from northern Africa and the Middle East to Europe, terrorism built a global media sphere, and after Donald Trump decoded the concept of conventional leadership. These changes bring us a global leap in output, or disaster. The new divider, a rapid change through a powerful metamorphosis in technology, artificial intelligence, robotics, and biotechnology will change our lives and provide a jump in global productivity. This catalyst will propel a permanent change in our societies, employment, inequality, and privacy for the elites and the middle class, banked and unbanked, while fresh water presents a risk multiplier, the seed-cause for every war in the Middle East. Water, a vital substance, will eventually run out in China, while the rising sea-level, in multiple ways, creates a global migration crisis.

Our societies have swiftly transferred from a third revolution of digital, to a fourth revolution of hyper-connected information, where the democratized technical ability for an individual allows remote participation for a cause, through influence, with leverage by social networks to change the global world order in our lifetime.

During my teenage years in heartland America, over the brink of nuclear winter in the 1980's, the West played well by pushing propaganda and influence through media of all sorts - computer games such as Missile Command, Defender, Centipede, toys like G.I. Joe, Real American Hero, Superman, Captain America, and the like. Motion pictures had, and still have, a powerful impact in youths and their thinking. Every generation enjoys letting go for a moment to enjoy the two hour setting of a James Bond spy action, or more serious and historically connected imagery such as Schindler's List. In the deep moments of the Cold War it was essential to fight for every second of media time and every thought in one´s mind to counter the adversary, therefore movies, such as Rocky, Rambo, and Top Gun and music of all genres, such as Bruce Springsteen's Born in the U.S.A, or Pet Shop Boys Go West, were essential in their time and still play a role today with their sequels and iterations, to manage and control how the world thinks and works.

In earlier decades there were numerous ways to interact and deliver pro-Western thoughts in a variety of formats; thousands of books, propaganda radio such as Liberty for Europe, and television broadcasts with TV series like MacGyver for superior technology, Dallas for the American Dream prosperity, and Miami Vice for tropical justice, all examples of primetime propaganda. After the evening thrill and restful night, print machines pushed out dailies and newspapers with slightly, or largely biased, stories for breakfast.

All of that consumed, filled with dreams, power, excitement, fantasy, integrity, and horror, but safely from the comfort of one's couch. But at the same time, everything evil had the word Soviet on it, and the visuals of a hammer and sickle were presented. While the Eastern bloc wasn't that good, actually rather clumsy, in sexy popular media, they did have some hits in the music scene and even created their own song competition variant called *Intervision* to compete with the *Eurovision* Song Contest. However, the socialist system never succeeded in creating tempting movies, but they did manage to have language courses on television in some European countries. The way the East charmed was with power through visual oppression, which eventually ridiculed the regimes that ran them.

I started writing this book in December 2014. First, I thought about the mediascape we live in and the synthetic truth that the media surrounds us. First they fill us up, to the level of exhaustion and fatigue, then obfuscates so we become confused and lose track, and eventually hyperbole and deprecate, by taking turns and then causing us to either justify, reject, or simply forget what really happened. And at the same time, present images are reintroduced as a shock, as needed, to present a trauma-of-an-image for a tertiary cause such as introducing or abolishing laws, governmental causes, elections, or simply for defense budgeting reasons.

Soon after New Years of 2015, I participated with the University of Turku in the American Study Groups classes that were filled colorful discussion. That gave a refreshed shape for the book and an in-depth background, but they also raised the bar to a new level by adding in a chunk of history, relations, media operations, and dimension. I decided to open up the 1980's propaganda section, to widen the first part of the book, defining in detail where we are and why we are here, in terms of societies. What was done right, what could have been done better, and why democracy is not the sole exclusive means for prosperous society, as we have learned from the success of China, bringing millions to the middle class and success they could not have even dreamed of two decades ago.

In today's world, we see a different mediascape, where the big four - BBC, CNN, RT, and Al-Jazeera, all try to charm and lure the audiences of their adversaries to their tempting version of the truth - their imagery and blended visuals intertwine as the world we see.

At the same time the human made disasters of the Middle East drive masses of refugees into Europe, causing distress in the European Christian majority, increasing divisiveness in citizen populations, identical to the journeys of desperate youths sent by their families for the chance of a better life from Central-American countries such as Guatemala and El Salvador towards Texas. The previous transportation method, Death Train, was closed by Mexican authorities where the refugees were evading checkpoints set by corrupted Mexican federal police. Meanwhile the version of a European mass exodus has switched from the traditional group of vagrants to a digital migration, where most individuals hold a smartphone with real-time communication of faced threats, dangers, and calamity of their peers among various borders in their journey towards a believed better life, a message relayed through imagery and experiences, reflected from actions taken by citizens, portrayed by local and regional medias. In America, the U.S. has outsourced the influx of masses to the Mexican government, compensated by an annual sack of dollars. In Europe, Germany traded-off with Turkey in a similar fashion to limit the Syrian refugee flow as compensation was made with euros, branded as aid and releasing limitations on Turkish citizens to allow visa-free travel to Europe.

These masses, in part, will assimilate to western values, but portions seeking to benefit from imported antisocial behavior, cause a negative view in their presentation in media. Estimates of new citizen volumes vary, reaching at least eight-digits, exceeding the point of stability of society in Europe and America. The local media of each country presents this as the largest mass movement since the Second World War benefiting the local politics, favoring increasing values of nationalism, leaving room for external plots and opportunism of populists. The masses of European audiences, a volume in hundreds of millions, are controlled and guided by a variety of medias, local and regional, causing power shifts and a power vacuum in European soil. This creates opportunities for corporations to expand or cut unneeded loss making operations, with multiple excuses and apologies, hiding their true management decided intent. Western media, being mainly conservative but profit-seeking, display newcomers such as Donald Trump in the United States and populists such as Marine Le Pen in Europe with an abundance of airtime, as audiences on both sides of the Atlantic demand their visual content increasingly in entertainment mode. The age of celebrity-politics meets mockery and jibe, shown as reality-show-delirium that is easy to dig into and become a follower of, expands the blanket non-stop craze to all media multiplexes in our everyday lives.

This book *reverse engineers* some of the tactics of how imagery and audio, perception and distance, and denial and obfuscation makes us believe things that did not happen, or at least not like how they were told in the twisted narratives and the reasons stories are presented to us as new, delayed sort of new, or a continuance of a series of new. These ongoing stories are then prefabricated and scheduled, while at times broadcasted as quickly evolving true actions.

I hope the perspectives presented in this book issue notions, opportunities, warnings, second thoughts, ideas, and even eye-openers. Coarse verbal language that politicians and leaders spit out, social networks mix, and corporates benefit from, escalates in times of non-consequence jibe presented without shame. One may ask, can we trust the society and the messages that nation-state administrations and corporate PR departments present for us?

SAMI LEINO

1. Who Believes in Western Saga?

Ailing America - Tailing Europe

In the 1980's, the western media ruled, leaving Eastern bloc leaders buried under strong rhetoric with clumsy presentation, the sex appeal of music and movies became a major driver for the West's benefit and was presented through popular culture in the widest meaning. Today, we live in another era, where all three competitors, the superpower America, magnate China, and hollow Russia, all have learned from their mistakes and missed capabilities of growth, decision-making, resources, and the complex modern society system itself, that in every large country is above its leader.

America has been surprised militarily twice; first, during Pearl Harbor in 1941, where the Pacific Naval Fleet was destroyed and second, on September 9th, 2001, a strike to the heart of the western commercial and business epicenter, the World Trade Center, where the healing is still ongoing. Today, America is technically stronger and more vigilant in crucial pieces of information coordination and internal sharing, the functions missing before the events of 9/11. However, America is at the mercy of fragile technology that can be pushed to a halt by clogged networks, neutralized sensors and collapsed software systems built in China. Processors hidden within adversarial architecture would cease operations in case of war, setting the United States at the mercy of the adversary. The air, land, and sea power of today's world have added two additional dimensions; first, space, not anymore a 'Reaganistic' dream but a true reality and a constantly equipped battlefield, and second, influence of the masses, persuasion that lures citizens, hundreds of millions of them, globally either for or against a multifaceted frontline with hacker groups, who would play a considerably larger part in any global conflict between the superpowers of China and Russia and the West; America and

Europe. Persuasion and lure of the masses, with soft power for the message sender's benefit, turn the tides between the belief of success or failure between competing forces; saga of the West, prominent China, belligerent Russia and rising India. Not forgetting newcomers Brazil and South-Africa as part of the BRICS nations. Upcoming countries in Africa and South East Pacific, including Indonesia with over 300 million residents and Nigeria with over 400 million by 2050 (1), will up the number of residents and industrial output considerably.

The United States, a nation that has 5% of the world's population and represents over 20% of the wealth on our planet, has lead the development of wealth, technology, liberty, and opportunity of the human race since the Second World War. But in the last 15 years, the nation has crippled itself, leaving the country in state of *vetocracy*, the term coined by Thomas Friedman, where neither side in parliamentary decision making gets to have matters their way, instead everything is vetoed until no party can progress in any critical matter. Out of vetocracy comes stagnation, as the country does not enjoy a functional leadership. This leads to a crippled state of no movement and the eventual loss of power itself. This has happened and continues to happen to the leadership of the United States in an increasing manner.

Since 2012 the second Obama administration has been unable to reduce critical items, such as the polarized political field, domestic instability between different ethnic groups, commercialized criminality increasing inequality, and the national debt and constant trade deficit of America. The hyperpolarization in Washington, where Republicans and Democrats are unable to work together, pushes the country to alter its society to prevent further divisiveness, maybe even change the way it elects the President and Congress. If all crucial parts were elected in a concurrent process, there would be unanimous decision making capacity and the country would regain its ability to gain momentum. One can ask if there is a structural fault in the mold of American society. Changes of this caliber are more of an illusionary vision than reality. If the landscape in Washington changes, nation around it would believe in the future again. Eventually demanding a change and accepting any result to alter the way the elite and insiders, who look at matters from the common man's perspective, run the country. These are the times where the opportunism of outsiders, social-democrats such as Bernie Sanders and billionaires like Donald Trump come into play with high field demand.

Populists and demagogues say things people think, but do not dare say. Americans are looking for alternatives that allow transparency of election funding and scrutiny of promises. The angst of the declined middle-class has been rising since the late seventies, clearly paving the way for unconventional outsiders to gain momentum in taking over the political leadership of the 2020's. The number of industrial jobs declined from 19.5 million in 1979 to 13.7 million in 2007, caused by profitable factories that produced appliances, vehicles, and electronics, moving their manufacturing to Mexico (2). The mostly non-educated middle-class of the heartland were left unemployed in deserted cities of the Midwest. The jobs themselves haven't disappeared anywhere, instead they have been recreated to Mexico, Taiwan, China, and other reduced cost labor countries. Taxpayers make investments into a democracy by deciding the leaders to guide corporations in their outsourcing campaigns. Should democracies penalize companies that outsource production to low-cost countries? The executive rewards became goal of corporate America in early 1980's, stealing the American dream from middle-class, which resulted a reality of outsourced jobs two decades later. The cost savings were not re-invested into education and industries, but to stock purchase buy-back schemes which adds into wealth gap and benefits major stock owners. These are reasons why new era of outsider leaders advance benefiting from the opportunity of fading middle-class dream.

New leadership intends to push aside the frustration that has filled the minds of tens of millions of voters, in the era where each voter can also be a writer, reporter, or a commuter between information stations within social media. Traditional leading medias allow commentary, a method to influence with short comments and referrals. Money still rules for buying television airtime, but the entertainment factor is gaining a stronger grip in choosing the leader for America. People want entertainment and are willing to stand up for someone that questions the current leadership model and elitist driven hegemony that has ruled for over a century in U.S. politics. People want their leader to be a person who they can proudly say are 'doing a good job.' The trust factor between citizens and a statesman, or woman, should be rebuilt by gathering the dispersed minds of society to aim for a common cause, which is far harder to do than to declare. The greatest leaders are raised to the podium by having people of various backgrounds stand tall behind a common cause. Very few individuals have this ability.

Think of the presidential election of 2020 where celebrities like Kanye West would produce a glitter filled glamour show, with previously unheard claims said out loud by an outsider, creating fandom in an unprecedented scale. Or the era with election of 2030 running Mark Zuckerberg with running mate Elon Musk. These would create realistic and verbally ample opponents for any traditional candidate. A presidential pitch for audiences in a rock concert manner, fitted with lyrics declaring the campaign message in repetitive mode, causing an earworm for listeners, and transforming audiences into publicists for candidate's message - the next step of celebrity politics, amplified with social media and reflected back to the audience itself.

The economic stagnation that started with the 2008 financial meltdown created deep polarization, then weakened both sides, the ones in power and the opponents in line waiting for their turn. This created a state of stall and polarization in the general political field and internally in the political blocks themselves which ended their ability to govern. America suffered from a political lack of capabilities to make changes in order to have the country pulled out from a 'vetocratic environment.'

The hyperpolarization of leadership in the United States has lead the people to anger and disaffection, severity and rage, in volumes, that compromises America's unity, but only silently, as major news outlets run a controlled media flow. Live events such as the Super Bowl are delayed for five to ten seconds to cut out any surprising breast flashing, "the nipplegate", something that Janet Jackson presented in 2004, outsmarting media leaders for public amusement. Most of the country feels that there needs to be a revolutionary change, to recreate how Washington is run, without disorder and mutiny combatting on national debt ceiling. Americans are looking outside existing political power and leadership for the next decades - with frustration for the elite running Washington.

The traditional power of gala dinners and TV commercials for fund raising still yield results for the runner's budget, but increasingly the direct means of fundraising is gaining momentum. Social media, on demand television, and guerrilla campaigns have proven effective in gaining targeted visibility among younger audiences in the 18-34-year-old range. Guerrilla campaigns can be effective when executed properly. Covert campaigns against western government personnel created and managed by guerrilla marketing agencies blended with leaflet distribution from a drone, above the city streets of an adversary, a silent outsourced hygienic campaign against adversaries can appear and vanish in hours. People's intention, motivation, fear, greed, consumerism, voting, and spending can be guided by carefully timed, planned, and well-executed campaigns regardless of their size. When influence building works in miniature scale for some dozens of people, it works for millions and hundreds of millions of viewers, the tricked ones. The money flowing into elections through new paths allows outsiders to participate without connections to traditional funding through "approved" channels. This has decreased the role of parties in the traditional sense. These channels for political influence, popularity in social media with exponential visibility and fame, allow direct communication between the runner-up and opponent. The traditional power establishment is left on the sidelines, outside the reign of the traditional political power struggle of the electorate.

References:

1. Wikipedia - Nigeria, Indonesia
2. Pierce R. Justin, Schott K. Peter, THE SURPRISINGLY SWIFT DECLINE OF U.S. MANUFACTURING EMPLOYMENT, NATIONAL BUREAU OF ECONOMIC RESEARCH, 2012

SAMI LEINO

Information as National Strategy

Information warfare can be seen as a multitude of influence waves, relentlessly washing our faces with violence and a constant conflict. The constant information warfare questions our system of belief, and intends to guide us towards extreme situations, to turn our heads the other way, away from the truth.

The great narrative of the West is picturesque but kept abstract with the intent to have a discourse with the global media scenery. The beautiful imagery collapses with photos from the prison of Abu Ghraib or when an Apache helicopter assaults the press with offensive instructions given in the evening main news, and causes an instant image crisis. Media cannot be controlled, content creators, broadcast companies and the viewers all make the news and take the content, process, relay, and discuss it with friends and colleagues. Even partly or fully machine written news stories can be tweaked to seek or present blame if the content creator so chooses. Information warfare violates our thinking and alters the mindsets, tempting us to take a side for or against a presented evil and adversary, as informational warfare is not won with proof or facts, as no one can be certain what those are with high confidence, instead battles are won in the minds of the viewer and how stories are perceived. It is essential to understand that how things truly are have no relevance, it's how they look in the vote-holder's view that matters.

Propaganda is a political version of influence building; it intends to distract decision-making and capacity to act in a society. Information warfare takes place between medias and has connections to nation-state operatives. These offensive operations are part of a larger hybrid warfare strategy, while it is the intent of the sender of the message to create covert operations that do not reveal political or administrative connections of the influence building. In democracy, lying is not illegal, but it is unethical, whereas in an autocracy and totalitarianism lying may save or doom, depending on to whom it is projected. The Western justice system demands the use of principal and discipline in warfare.

Influencing social movements to react and respond, are essential themes in cyber-warfare, to sensor out what's going on in adversary's mind.

After the events of 9/11 when World Trade Center was destroyed in Downtown Manhattan, the Bush administration struggled to organize and systematically convey the imagery of a national trauma. Domestic and world audiences were influenced by the US administration driven strategic approval for promotion of American democracy, with three wars in two generations. As in the 1950's and in the midst of the Cold War and beyond the Reagan era, the winning of hearts and minds has been essential for influence, using soft power to soften and disintegrate possible adversarial thoughts by nations and their armies. Despite the super power status, America needs support from its allies to maintain its success globally. The western liberal democracy and its welfare generating economy has stalled for over a decade, people in their stagnated economy question the western model in general: Is the established democratic model, the promised western saga still valid? While building the American outlook for decades, the flickering approach, creates an unethical and unconstitutional resonance among U.S. citizens living in an expanding inequality. Preserving democracy with immersive mass persuasion, US tactics can be seen as sometimes immoral and callous. While counter propaganda paints America as a distasteful, unipolar, authoritarian despot (1). A carrier strike group is how the United States sees itself. While adversary notices an opportunity of high propaganda value to sink one. Being the symbol of hard power and national pride, the U.S. usually does not cow in the face of a crisis. Nearly every administration seeks an alternative solution from the nearest Nimitz-class-carrier to unwind diplomatic issues or to bring down a delusory dictator. The strategic influence is built with politics, soft power, advocacy, diplomacy on the public stage, and the respect and cooperation of allies and neutral countries instead of oppressive maneuvers. Reagan's initial national security strategy contained four basic components: diplomatic, economic, military, and informational.

In the 1980's, information was noticed, and elevated from a supporting instrument to a top element of national strategy. This emphasis on information and the psychological component, strategic influence, of the national security strategy continued throughout his presidential terms, and still evolves further today.

Carter was a good president with a bad luck. He came to the White House to bring in clarity and sanity after the early 1970's havoc of Nixon's paranoia and the Watergate scandal, the oil crisis that allowed the Middle East to influence Western economies by adjusting prices in "everything oil." At the same time the Soviet Union made great progress in tying up United States in the nuclear race, and even passed the U.S. in late 1970's with their SS-20 missiles, the doomsday machines, that the Soviet leader Andropov was eager to use until he was on his deathbed in 1984. At the same time the Shaw got overthrown in Iran, the Caribbean and Central America started to turn red, with all that causing a loss of belief in the West and its well-being, might, and positive dynamics that brought the level of living to such elevation that each generation could reach and exceed the American dream of previous generations. Carter was soft and adjustable, a negotiator, rather than a war wager. But in that time, with the East pressing on with the Warsaw Pact military alliance, in the United States many thought Carter was too soft to stand up for U.S. might and values – individualism, progress, change, competition, dynamics, materialism, happiness, and liberty. The similarities from Carter's era to the Obama administration can be noticed, though both clearly presenting two different eras.

At the same time in America's social studies classes, in 1983, after the pledge of allegiance to the U.S. flag, a teacher advised us to "go for Reagan, because we need someone strong," regardless of the odd time and place for a political speech, she was right in her way. Once elected from the underdog position as he was, there was toughness, strength, and the promise of a better life. There was even glamour in a modern way that some were concerned about because of Reagan's Hollywood background, as Ronald Reagan was the Frank Sinatra of U.S. politics.

Carter was an agricultural oriented engineer that became a statesman; many things that had been prepared in his time came into fruition in Reagan's era. This wasn't realized among younger generations when us students were watching the space shuttle Columbia take off on April 12th 1981 or when it landed at the nearby White Sands missile base a year after, a reaction-result chain of events seems very clear. While Carter was a diplomat, Reagan came storming in like an F-14 Tomcat at the time, with his "Evil Empire speech" that the global balance needed on March 8th, 1983. Russian President Vladimir Putin was at this very time in a class of a red-banner-school of the KGB, looking at the world from the opposite angle, overseeing the mistakes that were made in the past, making sure they would not be repeated by him and his classmate league of friends of the time, as we can convincingly visualize today by the distribution of the global Russian broadcast channel RT. After Reagan, the U.S. experienced a longer era of experienced presidents, such as President Bush, who was a younger professional politician, a businessman, ambassador in the United Nations, Head of US liaison office to Beijing and head of the Central Intelligence Service (3). President Clinton, a professional politician as well in the hey-day of the 1990's after the faltered Soviet Union, enjoyed high economic growth and ever rising stock indexes of his tenure. Many of the U.S. Presidents have been attorneys, a benefit in professional career. President Carter was born in 1924, in the small city of Plains in Georgia, a two-hour drive to Atlanta. He started from countryside to technology studies, then applied and was accepted to the U.S. Naval Academy and also graduated with a degree in nuclear science – a well-educated man. When his father died in 1953, he retired from the navy and returned to manage the home ranch, setting up a start-up company, a wholesale trade of agriculture products. The business flourished, his wealth developed well, and on the side he also participated in the school board as the chairman of the parent-teacher association. That pushed him onwards to local political positions.

In 1962 he was elected to the Georgia Senate. He was the

governor of Georgia in 1971, and decided to run for the presidency in 1976, two years before the election, which still isn't that common today even though it feels that every election starts earlier than the one before (3). This puts the presidential-hopeful under a microscope while running for the Oval Office. At the time, social media didn't exist, so the medium was television, radio, and printed press. Today social media is a personal two-way media channel to preferred audiences, a global self-branded newspaper for everyone to read, with sender-adjusted focus, without the business losses (4).

Social media presents common people as visible and clearly noticeable targets of influence, who evade the earlier gatekeeper model, where media and its press were easier to control and monitor the information they present. The matrix of influence has broadened from earlier decades of elites towards a broad range influence for the masses. Media warfare brings battles from fields to living rooms and onwards to minds. Typically, social media is a two-way street, the messaging can be mainly from the nominee to voter, due to the huge volumes of regional and national audiences. To present a perspective of the candidate charisma on TV was essential, as it still is today, but with a more dynamic and even radical approach to many open questions in society. Although today, the messaging is done through all social media channels, Facebook, Twitter, image centric sites like Instagram, discussions on WhatsApp, and of course YouTube, and Periscope, a broadcast app for smartphones - all the various parts need to be in sync with broadcast television and print media, which still bring in the premium visibility.

Social media echoes in real-time positives and negatives of the campaign rhetorics, and the campaign management team neutralizes the negatives for their own candidate, limiting the loss of approval. They amplify the positive vibes to maximize profits, to the sequence of events knitting them into an adaptable campaign message, unified and simplified for the masses according to sayings babbled out form the talking head itself. Opponents urge on the opposite messages and views, presenting him or herself with a positive cheer while the negatives of the opponent were sincerely presented in earlier decades. The difference between past and present lies with the multiple waves of information that is delivered versus the once a day message burst of past decades, with a reality television like constant drama that viewers find entertaining. This is only the beginning of a new era, celebrity politics, with glitter and glamour, the dramatic delirium of a show that the political environment will turn to slowly but steady, a process where traditional evangelical audiences and liberal views collide. While Gerald Ford was never elected as President, rather he was issued the job, due to Nixon's scramble and paranoia before and after Watergate, Carter presented a clean table, a solid background and clarity in general. Carter was an honest, pro equality, and Christian person, who hadn't been tarnished by Washington's sometimes sketchy and dodgy politics and dirty play. Ford didn't enjoy true public support; he had pardoned Nixon as first act in office. While the Soviet Union was living in a stalled era of Brezhnev at the time, the United States was ailing and needed a clear leader with public support. At least part of the American public felt ashamed and contrite after Watergate, many were confused about the events, at least the TV figure Archie Bunker was, in the popular television sitcom at the time, All in the Family. Media back in the day was limited and if you didn't trust it, the alternatives were limited. The national pride that fuels America, progress, mobility, and change, was occasionally missing in 1970's and that was dangerous for a global superpower, with the Soviet Union at the same time penetrated deep into Western politics, the KGB was looking into western corporations and stealing everything that could be copied and delivered to their motherland. Carter presented traditional values that a great portion of Americans still rank high today. He won by a landslide in 1976. Walter Mondale, Carter's vice president from Minnesota, originally from Norway by grandparents, and a lawyer by profession, supported Carter well (2). But lost in 1984 to Reagan, who successfully ran for a second term. Carter, unexpectedly, gave a personal, well thought note to some of the ambassadors at their inauguration, focusing on the ones that were next to the front lines of the Soviet Union, in the neutral nation states such as Austria, Finland, and Sweden.

"If you ever have anything that you would like to come into my attention, do not hesitate to contact me. If you need my personal help, regards to relations between our countries, come forward and talk to me." (2)

Jimmy Carter at ambassador inauguration 1977, White House, Washington D.C.

Carter's challenges started to pile up with foreign relations, in multiple ways, and eventually in such volume that one might conclude he was simply luckless. His term included the Iran hostage scandal that ended up in the globally televised humiliation of the United States. Operation Eagle Claw, where the Delta Force American commando rescue hostage operation, to free U.S. Embassy hostages, went wrong from the beginning in April 1980. This debacle ended in eight lost American lives, and the eastern bloc "reaped the press rewards" of the time. The U.S. was more successful with the 1980's invasions of Panama and Grenada. Again in George Bush's term in 1990 the Delta Force operation failed in its assault in Mogadishu where 18 Americans died, five of them Delta Force members, this time CNN presented the live broadcast from the East African coast bringing us into real-time war operations viewed from the safety of one's couch, the optimal place to choose, for better or worse, popularity politics. These events were also produced as a movie, Black Hawk Down. Back then and today strategy and intelligence gathering correlates directly with risk and casualties, and operating without intelligence pushes that risk even further. For the United States it is essential to brand its warfare with terms emphasizing ethics and distribute message with pop culture and general media with a declaration of a God-given right to revenge. Russia marches on with maximum visual destruction and presents every activity of violence as a defense of Russian interests and territories to its people, no matter how far out they may be from their actual borders. Technology has become the western ideology and identity of branded ethical warfare, for public approval is essential that the West has the intention of doing something good in the wars it battles, while the rhetoric's of precision weapons remove the burden of moral hazard for the public. Russia does not have this public burden, the more vengeance the better. Whereas the United States and the West are under constant pressure to not get caught breaking ethical standards, the terminology of operations and precision strikes smooth the media's appearance of the Western acts of war in the media.

Israel and Egypt agreed on a truce at Camp David, mostly due to Carter's influence on both. Anwar Sadat and Menachem Begin signed a peace agreement at the White House to end the 1967-1973 conflict where Israel had been attacked by Egyptian forces in response to a conflict over territory. As a man having in-depth knowledge of nuclear physics, Carter took careful advancements to limit proliferation of nuclear weapons. He was publically present to the full extent, setting his leadership and political weight behind the effort through press, and had the SALT II agreement signed (2). The challenge for America is that while a Republican leader consumes national financial capabilities in two terms, a Democratic one is needed to balance the situation out in the next two terms. A Republican method responds promptly, even with offensive measures. The Democratic method is to cooperate and stabilize, to heal with natural herbs and an ameliorative approach with a seamless outcome, whereas Republicans want to treat the patient with radiation, invasive surgery, and shock therapy.

As presidents, Barrack Obama and Jimmy Carter were healers and men of peace, the brightest statesmen of modern times, but both experienced a change in momentum, first for them, then against their fame, as their tenure came to end. Eventually the United States needed someone strong, to make the West win again. Ronald Reagan took over the helm and steered the West to victory over the Cold War opponent of the Soviet Union, but with many of Carter's plans and ignited incentives, that flourished a decade later, again both kinds of treatment, soft and hard power, were needed for an optimal outcome.

One can think of the necessity of a democratic - republican cooperation and reciprocity, in the terms of leading a flock of birds migrating from one end of a continent to the other. The migration happens annually, whereas the presidential change happens every four to eight years. With the right leader in both teams, the nation wins. But with a two term delay United States quickly distances itself to a drifting nation that simply sits by as Russia and especially China rip-off personal information of citizenry, research and development achievements, relations of who knows who, financial and even medical records. Would they deliver a cyber-attack, if the scenario would be the opposite? The United States may have slid into an asymmetric war with China and Russia through media and cyber influence, without acknowledging that itself. If a confrontation is evident and there is no way out, the one making the first act can gain an advantage. In various cases of foreign politics, if the United States intends to solely use the soft power of its international security policy, it is seldom willing to start actual war operations. This may change in a post-Trump era, as the soft power equals a no result syndrome, that has been prevalent in American politics since 2008, comes to an end.

Times have changed since 1990's. Neutral countries belonging to western block carry identical burden of rhetoric in foreign policy to their fellow NATO member states. There is no feedback of military assets as a safety net for neutral party, which results in not that clever way to operate a country. Socks, pants and bread are not enough in modern warfare, where operative campaigns last hours rather than months. In 2020's nations belong to an alliance; West, East, North or South, or they slide inevitably towards influence of a regional strong arm nation. States rely on large global operator's credibility and foreign policy such as US.

In America, often matters throughout the country are driven to the extreme, the train doesn't stop until it hits a terminal wall of consequences, bankruptcy such as Enron, or government bailout like AIG and Lehman Brothers. Or the opposite, procrastinating, without realizing that other nations or hostile groups have overtaken, as happened in the 9/11 terrorist attacks. The drifting roles of the United States and European Union present a threat to the West in general. Europe still mentally and blindly relies on the United States to save Europe economically and militarily, whereas

Washington has quietly stepped back from Europe in the aftermath of 9/11 terrorist attacks. Leaving Europe, at least partly, in a power vacuum, raveling geopolitical divides, for the current generation, while the United Nations has declined in their ability to disassemble conflicts globally (2).

Reference:
1. Jantunen Saara, Infosota, 2015.
2. Iloniemi Jaakko, Vallan Käytävillä 1999.
3. Kissinger Henry, World Order, 2014.

4. Donald Trump , March 2016 Presidential campaign

Carter's false choices with Panama and Nicaragua

Panama was originally built on Colombian soil, where the United States had built a channel and defined it as a special governance territory. This was a strategic asset, for obvious strategic reasons the U.S. wanted to keep a say in the area, but Carter needed to transfer the channel to the government of Panama. The country of Panama was actually created to have a US channel there. After a long quarrel, Carter's idea to transfer the channel to the government of Panama won by a single vote. In earlier decades if any risk would have arisen around the Panama channel, the United States would have intervened with force without hesitation.

In our times, Nicaragua's channel project with China in the 2010's is actually a dock for the Chinese naval fleet for maintenance, some hundreds of miles from the United States southern border. China is also building an airbase and in the longer run, the Chinese missiles will have a fly time to any U.S. city in 10 minutes or less from Nicaragua. Reagan would have had a strong stance and opposed it, even with force if needed. Why would the U.S. allow a strategic transfer channel to be present in its backyard with China's navy?

Media disaster in Teheran

Iran was not only a bridgehead to the Middle East on the eastern front; it was also a key location for a United States military base with a considerable amount of US personnel and equipment. Iran was a prime spot to monitor Russian internal radio traffic and monitor the Russian space program and nuclear testing. When Ayatollah Khomeini, the religious leader, moved from Paris back to Teheran in 1979 things went quickly from bad to worse for the West, not to mention Carter. Reza Pahlavi scaled down being a political underdog in his country. The 2500 years of continuous monarchy ended in February 1979. The modern secular Iran was flushed down and Reza Pahlavi had to flee his country and live in exile in Egypt where he died the following year. The Iranian people took hold of the United States embassy in November 1979. It wasn't an embassy building per se. It was a section of Teheran with parks and blocks of buildings. It wasn't students who penetrated the embassy, that was disinformation given to West, but they were an organized and systematic force, men without insignia, backed by conservative religious forces led by Ayatollah Khomeini, which eventually became the foundation of the Iranian Revolutionary Guards.

Delta Force troops got into a heavy sandstorm in the spring of 1980 when trying to rescue the 52 hostages. Carter's bad luck endured. Americans reacted; their leaders could not control and defend their country as a major player in global politics and defense. America was humiliated and presented as weak through the global press. The Egypt and Israel peace treaty had strategic value as the Panama Canal was lost and nuclear weapon treaties were enforced with Russia, pushed onwards by the United States as the nuclear lead that had existed since 1945 disappeared. The following 444 days nailed the end to Carter's presidency (1), as Algerians and the Swiss acted as middlemen between the hostile parties. Nuclear talks could have been done at later stage if at all, the sandstorm in the Iranian desert was pure back luck, but all the events and decisions were portrayed as a failure by the media and that opened Carter's administration up for judgment. In Christmas 1979, as a crown to the fiasco of Carter's presidency's failed foreign policy, Soviet forces invaded Afghanistan, aiming to approach and influence the ever-lasting oil resources of the Gulf States via Iran. Iran accepted the offering from Carter's administration due to the threat of an uncontrolled situation with Reagan's upcoming inauguration and possible change in the terms of the agreement. To thwart the Soviet's advancing attempts, this was a top strategic priority for the United States, a cherry topping to Reagan's nomination at the time.

'We need someone strong, Reagan is our man.' Teacher in our social studies class - Texas, 1983 (2)

Reagan took over and a new era of 'tough stance' started. To get the hostages out from Teheran, the United States had to free 8 billion dollars of frozen Iranian funds. Iran was also left with top tier fleet of Tomcat F-14s that America had offered with friendly terms just some months before the coup de état. The jets, the predecessor of the F-15, were the air superiority fighters of the day, so this wasn't a nominal discussion in the White House at the time. Back then the Soviet's infiltrated into western research of every field. Today's Chinese research and development have carefully and successfully probed into the United States latest thrust technology by stealing the blue prints of the F-35 well before it was off the line for tests, offering full knowledge of the latest engine technology the United States can offer.

Current day Russian leaders, derived from that era, process the same questions and challenges of land grabs and geo-strategy and act based on them, to the capabilities they have available. The current Russian security organization driven regime of the Kremlin approaches the Mediterranean Sea through multiple directions. They have learned their lessons from the 1970's and 1980's strategies, public relation victories and mistakes, with the aim to rebuild the identical sphere of influence and re-establish the Soviet era nation state and political borders. Meanwhile America is taking furlough from three wars it has tunneled through in two generations. America needed Reagan's double term to spend the Soviet Union to death. If the United States had idled for another decade in the 1980's, as it did in with its foreign policy in 1970's, Russia wouldn't have fallen with the Eastern bloc in 1990, but rather in the next millennium.

Reference:
1. Iran Hostage Crisis
   https://en.wikipedia.org/wiki/Iran_hostage_crisis
2. Author's personal experiences.

Hyperpolarization and Stagnation

The West lives with a revolution of leadership, something that allows a new breed of people to run things, instead of lifelong political self-guarding incumbents to run matters as they always had been. The revolution that effect changes throughout the systems in our societies will pave the way in the decades ahead. From 2000 onwards, the kinds of *voodoo politics,* defined by Laffer Curve (1) – if taxes rise beyond certain level this discharges growth in economy - will process people in a susceptible manner until there are no people to process. Nearly every institution, from parliament to tax collection and from social welfare to defense contractors, have been controlled by plutocratic forces that have ensured their well-being creating an elite that stagnates the ability to make decisions and progress in general.

Business leaders are used to everyone coping with their decision-making, not leaving much room for compromise or accord. In earlier decades one could lose alliances internally within parties, but in today's world those past alliances are disintegrated fields of people who may have such different mindset on essential political topics, that they could have a party of their own. Future leaders say things that aren't supposed to be said in live broadcasts, do things their way, distancing themselves from the traditional way of thinking and acting. In other words, future leaders do not care what the past generations think of them. Their fandom depends on younger generations who consume the multitude of media information and opportunity to follow people who they find exciting, talented, successful, capable in multiple languages. Who operate on an international scale and arenas, where messages obfuscate and 'hyperbole' to a level that always sounds better than they actually are in real life. Life is changing towards a future that is automated, where there is knowledge of everything and it will eventually be available as "Google connected in brain" (2), a constant connection, with collaborative decision making. Collaborative thinking will enable exponential capacity to understand on a higher level. In the 2030's this can all be reality, and the nation that understand the opportunity can lead in the global race. Better control of crowds, groups, and electorates in a vibrant environment of mentality and sentiment of predictions with real-time decision recommendations, drawn up on leader's dashboards from machine-processed information, cracked out from global data lakes that gather information from trillions of sensors globally. The one who has the best media and information system to influence, wins the game of global race, 'to whose story to believe in.'

Future leaders are transformational, disruptive, self-promoting extroverts, who possess charm to gather ultimate the team around them and understand in-depth how media works. Regardless of who wins elections, the age of hyper-connected societies prefer individuals with strong self-promoting skills, inventive minds that are able to innovate with cutting edge skills, an entrepreneurial mindset, to lead nation-states and corporations with constant change. The times we live in prefer amusing, entertaining acts that provide us escapist moments from our lives full of routines. In classic terms, if a person is too far-off from the center frame of agreed common values and norms of society, the society labels the victim as plain crazy. However, humans as a species still evolve from Homo sapiens to *Homo Evolutis (3)*. Our brains are able to slowly adapt in absorbing more information from the multichannel information world where we live today. The world today is created with exponentially more information piled on top of the information received and processed yesterday. Our thinking further evolves to cope with the complexities of relations in everything we experience daily. The younger generations allow more deviation from the traditional center of activity, they connect with people who are different from the traditionally approved framework of thinking, presentation, acting in their public social mask, and be detached from the main system of culture as needed. People that differ from the common group and a particular set are preferred as leaders in the lead-follow culture of our times. This creates an even stronger need for statesmen and women to present themselves as entertaining heroes of sorts. Act as leading celebrities for their nations and people, their cultures, who may be laughed at by looking from the opposite side of the border fence. In future elections, being a self-promoter and coming into a leadership position will require talent in acting, self-promotion, self-aggrandizement, hyperbole, celebrity everything mentality, and eventually, it does not hurt to be 'demagogic' of sorts.

Reference:

1. Laffer Curve – Wikipedia

https://en.wikipedia.org/wiki/Laffer_curve

2. http://www.ibtimes.co.uk/ray-kurzweil-human-brains-could-be-connected-cloud-by-2030-1504403
3. Enriques Juan, The Next species of Human
https://www.ted.com/talks/juan_enriquez_shares_mindboggling_new_science?language=en

Entertainment Politics

Today's political narratives play a mash-up of celebrity politics and the act of winning, with the main driver of this stream being Donald J. Trump, who presents himself as the new hope for America. The new Reagan of sorts, can be seen as "toughness meets celebrity hyperbolic narratives", but without Reagan's kindness and wisdom presenting speeches. Donald Trump offers simplified straightforward solutions to problems, with a "let's make America great again" theme. He uses the words us and we, and they and them, according to the rules of influence creation, presenting a setting of *us* against *them*. Mass persuasion with direct guidance is a simple product, easy to understand and psychologically to *purchase*, the only cost being one's *acceptance*.

Our border is like Swiss cheese, people come and go.. we have got to change our thinking. - Donald Trump, March, 2016

Reagan had his career in Hollywood, acting in television commercials and motion pictures. Donald Trump has been the lead for over a decade in the Apprentice TV series, searching for a business tycoon, presented around the globe. Both of them, Reagan and Trump created part of their wealth and credibility from scratch, in line with the ideology of the American Dream, the self-made-men of their time. The power of unlimited media visibility and cash allows Donald Trump to say things as he pleases, things other people think but do not dare say, whereas Reagan's model of the power, and its delivery, was relayed through a simplified message that the adversary and public surely understands. Such as the Axis-of-Evil speech held in March 1983, after the Soviet Union had intentionally shot down the commercial airliner Korean Airlines Boeing 747. A fact revealed a decade later, Russia edited the communication recordings from "the airplane lights were blinking" into "the lights were not blinking" as this was crucial for international community in understanding whether the airline was a commercial flight or not.

Reagan, an underdog, who no one gave a chance before the 1981 elections eventually came and he won the election for the White House. Trump-era and Reagan both face a similar situation with foreign policy and security issues which were handled softly.

Questioned national credibility status and foreign politics of their times: ailing America, rising Russia but now with a new twist, quickly emerging China. In 1980, Reagan was first overlooked, then calmly feared, and eventually hailed. Reagan caught up to Carter in polls, as Trump battled Clinton 35 years later. History does repeat itself, but every time with a different perspective and approach.

Regardless of a presidential candidate, people find amusement in the runner up's say, no matter how hair-raising their comments may be. Donald Trump excelled in this media space by issuing statements that normally go unheard in public speech, defining a new era of pre- and post-Trump, the unconventional newcomer. Trump is actually an entertainer with relentless courage in business affairs, who media reassembles and echoes, and who enforces the brand that the magnate and his close family present. The brand spearheads the business, enforcing a cult of the ultimate self-made-man, the American dream. Half the nation wants to support Trump's self-made-wealth, while the other half feels compassionate discomfort, even embarrassment. Nonstop television drama-comedy with Trump and his family-team in the White House is something that could make the world forgive America for its wars in Iraq, bringing the US back to center of audience approved global media imagery. Some Democrats claim that he would give the country a bad reputation, but the freedom of speech trumps loud-mouthed talk and Trump proposes any difficulty is met with a simple solution; Trump. In European countries the thesis has traditionally been minimized in media exposure, but increasingly Europe is having its own presence of ultra-rightists and leftists, Marine Le Pens of France and Nigel Farage's of the UK. Populism simplifies reality into villains, opponents and the rest of the people. Meanwhile in Russia, President Putin, the power holder of the essential media channels outright, decides who is presented and who will eventually win the election. In Russia, the media owner agrees with the state, or local media companies face a cancelation of the permit to operate.

The new leader portrays himself as the savior, the daring leviathan for the people who are fed up with the elite, the silent majority of middle-class white- and blue-collar population, who do not usually vote. The silent portion of the nation wants to have their say on the ridiculous never-ending law suites, "racist everything", and a healthcare system that possesses a structure that the nation cannot afford, depending on who one asks from. Presidential hopefuls act as the mouthpiece of the forgotten mainstream middle class, and every minority group, returning America to its greatness and respect without discussion about how these goals would be achieved. The financial independence of government debt that actualizes America's relationally weakened power to China is also one of the presidential media aims. Obama's foreign policy is about intelligent soft power, while Trump's is about imposing a direct, simplified power projection to solve any problem, whereas Hillary Clinton emphasis on NATO cooperation with partners at all levels being important. Trump's outspokenness was similar to Reagan beating Carter, when Americans demanded a better life, a thesis the nation was built on. Obama politics promised much, but delivered little partly due to tug-of-war at the Capitol.

"A recession is when your neighbor loses his job. A depression is when you lose yours. And recovery is when Jimmy Carter loses his." - Ronald Reagan

Regardless of the outcome in Trump's White House bid success, he has broadened his media exposure to such a level that he cannot only be defined as one-hit-wonder from the TV show Apprentice. Rather he has added credibility and gained a positive presence in the minds of approximately a third of Americans, which accounts for roughly 44 million households (1). If Trump wants to make more money, branding a household appliance "Trump approved" would see it selling millions of units. He presents an entertainment factor that people want to see when they turn on their television sets or stream video on the web. Regardless of his personal political fate, the items and issues he has placed on the table won't disappear or vanish from society. Quite the opposite, he has paved the way for the next celebrity enticed candidate to march their show towards the White House, in the post-Trump era of entertainment politics.

Reference:

1. Wikipedia – Number of US households, 133 million.
   https://en.wikipedia.org/wiki/List_of_countries_by_number_of_households

Credibility Factor

Identity branding mashed up with corporate like statesman leadership describes current day leadership. *Celebrity-leaders* such as Donald Trump and *political-leaders* Hillary Clinton and Chancellor Angela Merkel, *nation-state-leader* President Sauli Niinistö of Finland and *monarchial-leader* King Carl XVI Gustav of Sweden, and an *autocratic-leader* of the Russian regime led by Vladimir Putin. This is part of a transposition science piercing through our societies with politics meeting entertainment with strong rhetoric. This approaches citizenry and persuades society with carefully planned media offerings. In Europe, where the continent failed in its approach to create a common unified European identity the United States of Europe, instead it ended up as a mashup of national leaders each offering their rhetoric disguised as interdependent pro-European unity. In regards to Merkel, the attempt of doing good in accepting millions of refugees into Europe backfired, and added more problems rather than benefitting the European-African relations. Russia benefited from the uncontrolled state of asylum seekers from the Middle East, a tool of influence, by altering routes of asylum seekers travelling through Europe to a variety of countries. In business terms, the cost of creating an opportunity needs to be less than the upside; otherwise there is no sense of intent for influence building. The world will see more of the Donald Trump kind of fame and success enticed celebrity outsiders presenting a straight talker message, rather than the traditional sedated personalities of the pre-Trump era.

60 years of political attack adverts in U.S. Television

Mass Persuasion   1952
"New Bus driver" Eisenhower Answers America

Pro McGovern anti-Nixon advert   1972
"This is about deception."

Pro Carter TV Ad   1980
"I can't image him (Reagan) being the president, it is too complex of a job"

Family Values   1981
"I gotta think my way" Convincing Viewers
"Ronald Reagan is not a man that I would want leading our country for any period of time."

Subjugation
Pro Bush TV Ad   2004
The voice claims a presidential race candidate; "he votes for and against any policy…"

Pro Bush Ad   2008
"John Mc Cain wants to continue George Bush's economic policy…"

Pro Romney TV Ad   2012
"Under Obama's plan you wouldn't have to work or train for a job. They just send you your welfare check."

    Reference:
    The Atlantic and livingroomcandidate.org
    http://www.theatlantic.com/video/archive/2012/09/60-years-of-presidential-attack-ads-in-one-video/262115/

SAMI LEINO

2. Influence in Modern Media Age

This isn't a popularity contest, or is it?

Modern conflicts are no longer about fighting states and gaining territory. They are more about effecting on identity of citizens, influencing the political decision-making process and gaining control over a person's sentiment. Worsening income inequality with an overall decline of the middle class creates a game of survival, a need for a financial buffer, for most individuals facing economic turbulence. In order for a national state to offer its citizens the opportunity to take entrepreneurial risks that spur innovation, basic tools such as education and healthcare need to be ensured. Our societies function as template frameworks for individuals to build-up their wealth from solid ground with high-quality capabilities to cope in the global race of nations. Eventually these individuals become members of families with either strengthened or weakened acceptance towards messages from outside attempts to win over one's mind.

In our era, celebrities project a powerful popularity among millions of people; they hold the power of their followers. Celebrities have an advantage, they are already well known, and projectile a positive visibility for their fandom. The task for a campaign manager is more about molding their fame into suitable messages designed for the target audiences and spread at the right time during the campaign matching politics, economics, race, and religion in real-time as the media presents them, providing solutions for the day-to-day problems of the common man. Elites controlling the media, living in high-income, luxurious surroundings, have distanced themselves from the actual problems that individuals and families face. Messages with a simplified short content appeal to common values that can be consumed by large masses. The nomination battle tends toward easy to understand, simplified messages. One can respond to groups and individuals in personalized tactics. Traditional broadcast television, the ads before a movie, or newspaper adverts lack this personal touch.

The masses feel betrayed by the previous administration, and want a leader who is the apprentice for oil industry, financial institutions, and military contractors. A celebrity, protagonist, with a strong appearance and simplified message to face the challenges, convey a story, and provide a cure for real life problems. A story that assimilates to traditional hardship for the common man, where a realistic dream of financial success never hurts. Donald Trump's ability to understand money making, media, concepts of social media and related strategy, celebrity appearance, and most importantly the rules of modern day media dynamics, blended with a showman's appearance, gives him an edge in his performance. While other candidates pay for seconds of prime time advertising, Trump gains minutes of viewer focus while people anxiously wait for his next move, as if watching a sequel of a TV drama instead of a traditional presidential election. It is all about attention and the ability to say things the viewers feel, but do not have the luxury to say out loud, either because of the judgement of society, stigma, or even criminal and financial liability. Trump says things that the common man is entertained by in a twisted way, and hits back at the political arena, the silent masses that feel they have no way to influence their leaders. Trump presents himself as savior for the masses, feeling the pain of unemployment, mortgages, raising kids, and being a wife or husband in modern day life. He is a 'truth-telling presidential hopeful', successful businessman or a bubble waiting to burst, depending on one's view.

Donald Trump is perceived as a disaster for the extremely wealthy, even though he is wealthy himself, because Trump brings independence to political leadership, which again leads to an unpredictable future for the super-wealthy families that factually run the United States. Power is transferred from super high net individuals and corporations feel violated as their influence is suppressed and forwarded to someone who is outside of the traditional norms of super rich life. Something that the American political scenery has not experienced before, and for them, is a train wreck in slow motion. A slide of power from the traditional power holder's grip of slightly over 150 wealth American families (1) to the unknown. On one single matter there is consensus,

Trump is the most controversial candidate yet to successfully fight all the way to the gates of the White House. As in the love-to-hate, backroom biting, competition drama The Apprentice, Trump is split into two characters; first, a new hopeful apprentice, the holy grail of the middle class, to bite back at the ones the lagging middle class feels betrayed by. Second, he is the promoter of the all-you-can-eat television, newspapers, and magazines, the controlled era of the media and politics. This is visible presence of power, the opposite of the beholders of the majorities in shareholder meetings of the world's largest media houses and consortiums.

The new era of celebrity-driven-tide has opened in American politics, rising from the age of reality television, enforced with the selfie-stick-narcissist-era of the modern day media behaviour. This is the opposite end from plastic, scentless, inoffensive, non-racist, something-for-us-all programs, fit for mainstream broadcast networks and their declining power. Separate from hyper niche audiences, delivery per request, any screen size, built-to-order, with the viewer's intention to rise above the noise media democracy. Trump is major news, even if he loses he still wins as his brand lives on and progresses further. Regardless of what he says, after him comes the long tail of everything - other politicians, influencers, ratings, events, funders, and big money. News networks turn to Trump as a sure shot to boost ratings when he gives a speech or holds an event. From the early 1990's, when Trump was positioned as Gordon Gekko from the movie Wall Street, a profit seeking day-trader in the real-estate business. He has come a long way presenting himself as a new, strong offer to fight for America's good, pulling the western world forward. Like the Monopoly board game, with a popular culture version, where each world superpower has a block of buildings, plans, and executes the sphere of influence to other areas in the world, as property expands in the board game.

Reference:

1. http://www.nytimes.com/interactive/2015/10/11/us/politics/2016-presidential-election-super-pac-donors.html?_r=0

SAMI LEINO

Peaked US Power - Past or Ahead?

The failed wars of the United States have weakened America's absolute strength in the eyes of its Western allies, and adversaries Russia and China. The economic decline that the US has suffered in terms of uncontrolled federal debt combined with the divisive and polarized politics have degraded US capability and credibility in the eyes of credit rating agencies and debtors themselves, especially China. However, the United States projects global power and an environment of money making and consumption, and the promise written in the spirit of constitution to live a happy life. For a country that has evolved over 240 years reinvents itself through the technology edge that once was a decade ahead of the world. U.S. is tackling global challenges ranging from a reignited half-hot war with Russia to expanding the influence of China in the Pacific.

Slavery tainted the 18th century, degrading the polished personalities of the founding fathers. In the 19th century there was the American Civil War, where the North occupied the South. The term united wasn't very common in those times. In the 20th century life was already better, but the two world wars left the western hemisphere struggling with the Soviet Union and the Cold War. It wasn't long after that the Cuban missile crisis was settled and the Able Archer NATO training nearly ignited a global destruction with the Warsaw Pact in 1983, that nearly caused last decades for the developed world.

The world wars drove research and development of technology to new levels, so life in general was elevated to new heights in terms of consumption and material goods. Women's suffrage was a great achievement in the 1920's, it lead to the nineteenth amendment of the constitution. Life was healthier, but millions struggled to make their living and survive the Great Depression of the 1930's. In the 1950's the United States' industrial power peaked, but the social roles of men and women still had much room for improvement, which evolved after birth control became commercially available from drug stores, the sexual revolution evolved, entertainment such as musicals, motion picture, and music thrived, and women received more visible roles in company boards and throughout the entertainment industry and television shows.

In early 1972 the Vietnam War ended, where over 58,000 soldiers were killed in action, compared to Afghanistan and the second Iraq war which had 6,500 fatalities in total, almost nine times the death rate. In the 1980's the internet saw the first glimpses in the military and universities, but cell phones were nonexistent in the early part and rare in latter part of the decade. 3D imagery created a new opportunity and understanding of the human anatomy. The era of precision-targeted drugs for cancer and other diseases, such as treatment for HIV and AIDS, started. Most households received personal computers by the middle of the decade. **The Cold War eventually came to its end with the fall of the Berlin Wall in 1989 and the final breath of the Soviet Union was taken in December of 1991.** The 1990's were the new roaring 1920's of the Clinton era. Economy strengthened and improved, we had modem connections to bulletin boards and Usenet discussions. First we "surfed" at the rate of 28K, then 56K, seemingly lightning speeds. But we had to wait another 10 years for broadband technology to take over in large scale. The events of 9/11 were a clear collapse of the nation's well-being, with the dot com boom in the hands of investors and company valuations going down, the 2000's did not start well, and with the financial meltdown of 2008 one can fairly say the decade did not end well either. Some cities and realtors claimed that housing prices would not return to the pre 2008 level in our lifetimes, an estimate which eventually was proven wrong as either the houses were torn down in the aftermath of unpaid mortgages or they were re-evaluated in the rising housing markets of 2010 and thereafter.

The 2020's are a new promise of a better life for the masses at the lower end of the demographic pyramid in the emerging markets of South-East Asia and Africa. The non-educated and unbanked citizens, many without identification, benefit from the era of democratized information and knowledge. As all of the world's information is now in everyone's hand, with a mobile phone designed in California, then produced and assembled in Asia, constantly updated with assorted information by Google in Silicon Valley, social media now truly represents the pulse of the planet. Oil prices are low and they will likely stay low to keep Russia from receiving a powerful edge of the reignited Cold War that's already half-hot in parts of Ukraine with an expansion of influence by both the US and Russia, as well as China on the South China Sea and Africa. And the same sex marriage was approved by the Supreme Court. Self-driving cars ready to drive as regulatory approval from the traffic commission of California is sped further. The United States is still the El Dorado of financial success - the star of liberty and freedom.

However, the US version of democracy is not the sole means of success for every country in the world, as Finland has proved with the world's best education system that creates nation-state leverage for innovation and productivity, and China, which has successfully brought tens of millions people into the middle class, something they could not even dream of two decades ago.

Is America only great in movies?

America and its people have a positive cultural-history of being portrayed as monolithic, showing unity as a solid group, which has been a clear strength of the nation. The world around U.S. changed from a world of blocks to a mix of messy societies. Democrats realized this and united separate voter groups becoming a 60/40 party. With the support of Latino, African American, Asian and Native American minority groups, the party now receives support from over half of the population. As children, like-minded people gossip about each other with whom to cooperate with and who to evade avoiding bullies. Republicans have drifted from a union builder to an outlier, evading political compromise and rejecting facts to today's society, being unable to renew themselves as a party. We live in a world of messy societies resulting from economic divergence, as the GOP dismissively holds to slipping grip of power. U.S. politics got stuck in a vetocratic stubbornness, unable to agree on core priorities of society preferring their personal competitions of power. Business oriented leader benefited from the era of political disintegration and presented himself as the solution for voters, becoming an opportunity rather than a liability for the party.

America's criminal system is a commercialized version of justice; it has become a hypocrisy of what it once was, liberty and justice for all. It is a system that reflects an unbalanced and brutal, primitive society that ensures a constant feed of human material into a self-promoting system of attorneys and commercially run prisons. Policing the criminal justice system is a reflection of a primitive society topped with biased bigotry. The U.S. police force wants to be respected and hates the negative attention, silencing debate instead of preventing overreactions from happening. Cost optimization for profiting does not always fit into human rights of a nation-state. Looking at the U.S. from the outside, it's a system of hypocrisy. No wonder people globally do not see and believe in the once great western saga anymore. The U.S. administration is willing to understand how the system downplays its citizens but the legal framework supports over the top punishment and increases criminality by tearing apart families instead of correcting malfunctioning citizens.

Barrack Obama has been a healer and a man of peace. But the United States as a country, with strong internal dynamics, lags in performance with such a leader, the country does not win any longer. As with Carter, who is one of the brightest statesmen of modern times, who had bad luck, the times changed, momentum was against Carter and eventually the United States needed someone strong to make the country win again. Eventually that happened, Ronald Reagan took over the helm and played a game of defense budgeting between United States and its Cold War opponent, the Soviet Union, to victory for West, not only through defense budgeting but leveraging the unlimited scale of popular culture for the West's benefit – from Hollywood motion picture studios and the music industry of London and Los Angeles, towards the frontlines of the Iron Curtain in Eastern European audiences, with musical messages such as the songs We´re The Kid's of America by Kim Wilde and Born in the U.S.A by Bruce Springsteen.

One can think of the necessity of a Democratic - Republican cooperation and reciprocity as taking turns in leading a flock of birds migrating from one end of a continent to the other. The migration happens annually, whereas there is a new president every four to eight years. With the right leader in both teams, the nation wins. Change - regression in leadership, length of term, or unbalanced ritual of power and the United States strands itself as an ailing nation that simply sits by as Russia and China rip-off the personal information of citizenry, research and development documents, as well as financial and medical records, reliving the old KGB phrase, "the world was going our way". The lagging, former unilateral, strong role of the United States presents a threat to the world order.

Reference: 1. Foreign Affairs, April, 2016.

System of Beliefs

In the Soviet Union the central theme of their deception was to make the adversary believe that the system was not communist anymore. Instead, the main intent of the propaganda from the Russian system is to make the West believe that Russia is a great power, with imperial conservatism in its concept. This thesis was derived from Soviet deception tactics, where objectives were turned around to present a regime that has dropped the idea of unlimited necessities, as defined by the Soviet political power system. The intention of the narrative is to make the opponent believe that the West would no longer see Russia as a threat. convincingly presented by Eastern propaganda. If that would be the new truth, hypothetically, one could believe that the transformation of the United States into a communist system would not be a threat, manufactured by outsider forces, or in today's world of reality, that the constant flow of stolen information from western research and development, as well as identity theft, towards China and Russia would not be a disruptive threat to the West in general.

The source of tensions between a block of countries can be seen as a game of influence. Where the influencer promotes the idea of a race, whether that is economic, militaristic, or technological, which is the principal source of suspicion blocking the friendly emerging relations. The acceptance or rejection derives from the idea that one's own actions, for example building missile defense technology, are the cause of such tensions. Once this is accepted by adversary, to seek ways to reduce tension and retreat from the belief that has caused the situation in the first place. Reduction in defense budgeting, which could lessen available resources, would eventually have measurable outcome in the message senders propagandistic benefit.

Disbelieving vs. Believing

Jeane Kirkpatrick, the former United States Ambassador to the United Nations defined atrocities as "the will to disbelieve the horrible." Expressions of "disbelievable horrors" and "taboo expressions", both in textual writing and visual imagery, are generally rejected by us humans, as mentality that destroys creative thinking and the expressive mindset of many. Some startup entrepreneurs even avoid reading websites with negativism and conflicts, wars and diseases related drama due to negative disruptive forces in creativity. One may claim that such an evasive worldview is living in a bubble. If an individual has financial independence for such, it is their right to live in a secluded world of future building, which is often quite productive for the creation of new concepts and even patentable inventions. Cambodia, Ruanda, and Nazi Germany were all too ugly to look at and it was easier to turn one's head in silent denial. Such events may also build up pressure for the community not willing to see the horrors, instead of rising up against them. Introducing themes in influence creation that clearly violate the level of unbelievable horrors, the narrative reaches a new level of normal, raising the bar of noticed alteration in the flow of media. When this happens in repetitive mode, within the scope of the news, audiences lose track of the level of horrors and eventually disregard such media events as the new normal. When the new normal is combined with strong, daily information flow, the time decay and volume create media erosion that eventually levels any event, positive or negative. Hyperbole and deprecation expand in social media exponentially, reach and blanket the new level of normal in media events, therefore bringing us noticeable events, while constantly raising the bar of mental alert. A system of belief, where the eyewitness becomes the perpetrator, as the blame is put on someone who was not part of a tragedy, but may have turned away either from misunderstanding, ignorance, or simple shock.

Human Perception

The analysis team in corporate HQ interprets competitor information into a framework to extract, connect, and comb for the lowest common denominator, size of personnel, divisions and products, followers in social media, and possible weaknesses and strengths in customer demographics and market share. Heavy clustered-server-farms, scaled-databases running in them, and a series of complex software systems with tailored portions of data modelling, crunch the data into information and knowledge for a conclusion that is a sequence of probabilities. This is then again estimated by multiple individuals, us humans, into a report, leaving portions out and emphasizing pieces, bolding and capitalizing text, inserting suitable imagery in parts as the people creating the desired report, see fit. Creating a view of conclusions for the decision-maker, the emperor of sorts, the head of a nation-state battling a global war of influence, a chairman of an oil-industry corporation employing 300,000 people facing constant problems in the Nigerian delta, or the CEO of a family owned bakery and the chain of coffee shops that constantly clashes under pressure from the family run company board, and the head of department at the ministry of defense that has hundreds of people working for her. They all battle the challenge of determining the validity of information fed to them by the middle management that contains their personal interpretation, likes and dislikes, of an individual, team, or a competitor.

Added flavors - False conclusions

The weak link is human perception and personal intent. What we the people define as true or false, by interpreting the information delivered to us by our senses, then comparing that information based on the "normality" that each individual holds as the typical way to function in our society. This model is vulnerable to disinformation. By increasing and decreasing the level of false information fed into such a media ecosystem of manually interpreted messages, a number of weak spots remain through the organization. Distortion by each individual in the process itself, the number of weak spots increases as the volume of an operation increases, eventually causing an influx of information that starts to obfuscate itself, lessening the probability of the conclusion being valid in the first place.

Us humans, we the people, like to be talkative, socialize verbally and visually through a multitude of expressions during lunch breaks, beside coffee tables, and the famous central exchange of rumors where people smoke, nowadays often outside office premises. Since we want to fraternize in good favor, we spice up, add flavor, and make up content that may have a portion of truth as a seed. It's the broken phone model, with everyone hearing the message differently and a transcription that, depending on one's mode, weekday, life situation, and variability in accepting ensure a continuance of discussions based on rumors that become stories. Then mashed up with gossip, eventually creating urban legends of sorts, an "hazardous person that once was," but in the real world never existed in the first place. Many of us live simple repetitive lives and find it entertaining to fill out the truth with parts of a rumor, then feed it into discussions with others, keeping the discussion entertaining so that we are accepted in the group. The chain of information and its related gathering is filled with weaknesses; interpretations, social connections, relations inside and outside of the organization, all analyze information for their personal benefit. In extreme cases, information is manufactured, evidence is created. The situation seen in the field that in reality never existed. "She´s probably also this, because once she was like that" all comes down to gossip, faltering truth at work, and intentionally evading truth of what really happened and why.

Some of us have more colorful and interesting lives than others, living within the traditional mainstream. People may perceive stories as pure lies, when told about the chain of events that differ from listeners way of life. In the late 2000's, there was a director of an advertising agency who told stories fairly openly of his life and daily lifestyle. The narrative was far from traditional; everything from watching satellites and shuttle launches with special made 20" lens-telescopes, to discussions with a huge parrot, a Kakadu, that lived with him. People thought that the person was rather mad, but in fact the director, who also ran departments in the ad agency, had all the bells-and-whistles he talked about, and being the very creative, quick thinker he was, his presentation of life was judged by his coworkers with a conclusion of person mental state. A person that sidelines far off the normality of society can be seen as odd, or even crazy. What is normality? It is what the masses believe in their general acceptance. Elites in a society live far off the mainstream life, and their secluded lifestyle is limited in view towards masses. The further off you derail from the Central Line, off to the last stop at Elephant and Castle on the London Tube Map, people may judge based on eccentricity or amusement as someone may appear of their personality. As Nicola Tesla, the iconic inventor of early 1900's put it, "the world is full of conformists," but the ones daring to live a unique life defy that notion of conformism and may have a laugh at how others perceive them. "Throw them a bone, something crazy in a work interview, such as; May I kiss all of you in this interview? and perceive how people see you" said a friend of mine when talking about work interviews and how he performs in them. No wonder he is unemployed. In everyday life, one can rapidly see if there is a real match between people, a laugh with wrinkles in eyes or an interpretation of disgust with opened-eyes, non-acceptance, or a slip-second moment of silence, a halt and a head pull back - the appalling rejection. Human perception easily distorts messages from the truth in an organization environment of built-in fear of acceptance. This creates an archipelago of mental gulags, which cause personnel to say nothing, or to join any internal theme to downscale a labeled individual to save face among co-workers, rather than to participate and bring true value towards the decision-maker.

A common misperception of mass persuasion is that the creators of influence and media charm would be creating an ideology, a cultural belief system, and the organized messaging would be intended to disseminate the related beliefs (3). This can be the case in some occasions, the operative tactics of propaganda can be seen as the elites of society creating an illusion, half-truth of a full truth, or a random mix of these to advance themselves and their organization, and to drive the overall balance of power for their benefit. In some cases, the elite may also convince their organization, personnel, and also themselves to achieve a common goal. The tactics often play around a pragmatic approach to problem solution, such as, how to regain a lost influence of power. The Kremlin's pragmatic approach and advance as far as possible, reflect the will and greed for power. After financial well-being has been secured, human nature tends to advance towards control. Politicians and corporate leaders especially may have a tendency for ideological power play; some claim this to be part of a survival skill set for portion of people (2). Persuasion, the antecedent of propaganda, dates back thousands of years. It started out as rhetoric, ethical and logical tools for arriving at the truth through reasoned debate. Then evolved into advertising, news, and reality television shows. Further to mass persuasion, where all these factors are combined with varying doses to create advertorials, as reference to documentaries. It can be said mass persuasion is a lighter way to deliver propaganda, which often is interpreted in negative connotations, even a dangerous message, and with intent to advance the sender's benefit. Mass persuasion can be seen and created by delivering a progressive set of waves, with a relentless force to overcome the adversarial mindset, for good and bad, negative and positive, of a person, country, sports team, competitor, government, or an organization in general.

In the 17th century Pope Gregory XV created the first known propaganda machine for the propagation of faith, Congregatio de Propaganda Fide (1). This became the first global dissemination of a message, creating a powerful force that even lead the cardinal to be called Red Pope. The message itself included everything related to uniformity of thought related to Catholism, its establishments of national colleges for the education of priests in the Old and New World. In today´s world propaganda is understood as altering the sense of understanding by manipulating mass politics and the views of individuals and groups for the sender's benefit. In the beginning mass persuasion was created to act as a weapon against non-believers, heretics, atheists, and pantheists, as the Church was afraid they would be challenged, as eventually they were by Martin Luther who had successfully challenged the Church in Western Europe. The Church at the time can be seen as the elite, a group that was well organized and had more resources and powers compared to individuals at the time. This can be seen as the informational society of those times. A mere comparison of the powers and relations and the wide gap in resources in those times, but also exist today between the common man and massive media houses of our times that disseminate their message in a coordinated fashion.

The spread of a message, propaganda, for the benefit of an organization in those early times was successful and efficient, which lead the Church to hold on to its power in much of New World, which became, and remains, widely Catholic. But in northern Europe, Protestants, who were active in the area, set up influential, informational societies and were able to hold on to their side of the story, their mass persuasion.

Reference:

1. Left Catholicism 1943-1955: Catholics and Society in Western Europe at the Point of Liberation
2. Graduate School of Public and International Affairs and Gordon R. Mitchell, Department of Communications – 2006, University of Pittsburgh
3. Keller, William W, Preventive Force: Untangling the Discourse.

Social Masks and Trait of Sisu

We have no consequences in our consequence-free society of social media (1). Citizens of any age and ethnicity can freely express their opinions in nearly every country in the world. Regardless of the internet not reaching everyone on this planet, most of us belong to some social media network. Even if you do not, there is always the possibility to comment fiercely in a moments notice, spurs of repetitive wordings, as a caffeinated retailer. Viciousness behind the scenes, anger, or even rage hidden behind a throwaway email address, posting, then running away chuckling. The exhibitionism that relates to our use of social media blurs the lines between the real, physical me, the commentary me with false courage, and the official me, the one present in places of work and study, with the physical mask of presence. We actually full fill ourselves with political courage that is shielded by social media, or simple anonymity. They both offer a mask of false sisu, with little or no shame. Sisu is a mental state of never giving up, being relentless, and the courage of an individual to break through any obstacle, traverse any handicap. It is the ability to get by and rebuild even though your house would have been 'bombed away'. Residents of Louisiana, after experiencing Hurricane Katrina, have a great deal of sisu.

Verbal language in our news broadcasts has changed since 2000 towards street talk. Resembling a coarsening culture, a disregard of verbal consequences, as there are none. Even if there were consequence, outrage and hail burn off in few days, as the volume of information increases constantly resulting in *infobesity* (2) as similar news topics are echoed from multiple sources constantly. Time decay of information wears off in days and in the future only hours. News cycles are undersized and our attention span is only seconds, as we jump from one topic to the next. People don't care about consequences in social commentary as we do not care about guilt and shame. Public discourse has degraded to a repetitive echo between individuals. Communication of our era can be misused by simplification, to empower listeners with gaffes, and present content in a refreshed mode of honesty. Past mistakes are presented as proof of a refurbished person, with neutralized negativity and consequences. Earlier our standards of decency were tighter to send emails, and submit messages of appalling humor beyond good taste. As with any information, seeing a constant repetitive flow tames down any topic, creating information reflux.

The culture of lack of references and critique towards sources of information is careless and blurs the lines between information and gossip, even hoaxes. Celebrity news becomes the news for many, escapism takes control of viewers' minds, and people want to listen and hear everything in an entertainment mode. A Finnish study (3) claimed only one percent of 13-15 year-olds trust false news sites, when information is presented in social media, visually the same as the user's typical experience, only a few teenagers were able to notice disinformation. When the tide of information starts to appear in volumes most viewers, regardless of their age live in the same information bubble, causing the message to strengthen and increase. Social media blurs the line of factual news, gossip, rumor, and lie. The same study found that only one-fifth of sixth graders could define commercial content from news. Wikipedia and well-known news sites such as Reuters, CNN, and BBC present brick and mortar stores of the news world, they have credibility, as they are present in our minds with a high trust factor. Constant swap from view to another in various screen sizes, blurs the line of the message sender's credibility causing information to become equal, for all age groups. Some may claim that younger generations could more precisely define disinformation from information, but this could well be the other way around. When we compare from the era before the web and after, it gives comparison value, the myth of a *digi-native* does not enable extra powers for critique. This must be a tough part of education programs. Credibility of presentation, valuation, comparison, and argumentation create major part of the news. References do play a role, but eventually those references end up somewhere, defined by someone.

Social media increasingly becomes a news delivery platform, but why do we update our lives in social media in the first place? We have the need to socialize but also to structurally define our lives, creating open diaries of our lives. This changes person's ego, as publishing one's life becomes part of the culturally accepted norms of operation. To get approvals and rejections, approach boundaries and setting personal limits towards connections. Being part of a natural way to interact eventually becomes a partial identity. Social media increases socializing in the work environment as individuals can post amusing contents and connect in the physical world instantly, with expressions. Professional social media can become a tool for specialization and knowledge. This changes commentary to social media and it also changes us as people, in real-time. Increasingly citizens in our societies disregard shame, a social restraint that controls how and what we say, present, and claim in society. Usually humans feel shame when exposed as liars or when cutting corners. We are seen as bestial and pitiless. Acting behind a mask that is immune to shame makes us capable of functioning above the commonly accepted norms of society. Some of us are walking the path moving towards the age of shameless culture of nonexistent consequences in media exhibitionism. Eventually only disgrace is remembered, for better or worse, or more often both.

Eventually we will all become evangelists of information in our specialties that we have interest for. Anyone focusing in a niche, either for full time business, profession, or sport, gathers knowledge in such quantities that it piles up for credible visionary vision. We have an increasing number of data based evangelists and star-eyed fools that see further out, in their specific field of knowledge. All of us will become exhibitionists in our preference of products and services. Information creates us such, as media becomes more prescriptive and artificial intelligence increasingly takes over our lives. For businesses this means meaningful decisions and less errors.

References:
1. Leibowitz Mark, New York Times, Feb. 17. 2016.
2. KPMG, Business in the Hyper-Connected World.
3. Vehkoo, Johanna, Yle.fi: Valheenpalajastaja: Sosiaalinen Media Sumentaa Kritiikin, Feb. 15, 2016.

Democracy - Affluence and Influence

There are two conceptions of democracy. One, where the society is such that the public has the means to participate in a meaningful way in the management of the leadership and therefore in their own affairs of information flow, freely. The alternative is where the public is barred from interfering with the means of information flow and where information is tightly controlled. Therefore, one could say that propaganda is to democracy what the hammer and sickle are to a totalitarian nation state.

Under Woodrow Wilson's administration (1) in the United States in 1916, the message to the public was "Peace without Victory." During the First World War the population was very pacifistic and did not want to get involved in the war in Europe. But the underlying fact was that the administration was committed to the war and created a propaganda commission, the Creel Commission, which had a six-month deadline to turn the public from against the war to a warmongering nation that wanted to destroy Germany. The Creel Commission, which took part in Wilson's war, contained intellectuals, who took pride in the propaganda agenda, to drive the public from reluctance to war mongering by terrifying them with fanaticism. This was done with an extensive propaganda agenda to demonize the adversary, where the tactics and content itself were created by the British propaganda ministry. The agenda was to control the intellectuals in the United States, who would then distribute the idea around locally. Therefore convert the country into a wartime, hysteric nation, from the pacifistic idealism that the country was in, to war driven, revenge seeking citizenry that the administration needed for their justified entitlement from the ostensible authority, the voters.

The propaganda driven by the state with the bi-directional support of the educated classes can have tremendous effects in a society, removing any friction that normally would arise, either from intellectuals or the deep-rooted citizens. The manufacturing of the consent of the people was the agenda for leaders, ranging from fabricated hysteria to victimization in Russia. The Kremlin publicly depicts itself as the underdog in the expansion of NATO and the missile shield that had risen on the bordering nation-states of Russia.

In America, "trauma-of-an-image" (2), the falling man, is a visual imagery of a white-collar male falling down head first from the world trade center during the terrorist attacks, one of the 2,977 deaths, and over 6,000 injured, on 9/11/2001. The Pentagon's Office of Strategic Influence created a narrative, a productized righteousness of hit back at anyone obstructing the United States. At the same time victimizing each of the +330 million U.S. citizens globally to gain support for operations in Afghanistan and Iraq that no one denied at the time. In propaganda communication there is the essential piece of *us* vs *them*. Them referring to those others who are depicted as the adversary. The opponent in conflict, dispute, or outright war, in a hybrid war sliding scale from minimal harassment, defamation, and immersion of information in local media to conveying half-truths with divertive turns to create a fog of obfuscated truth. Something that ends in intentional confusion. This intertwines with cyberwarfare that hacks into financial, energy, broadcast, and communications networks causing a total loss of operational capability and knowledge of truth for the masses, a society-lost-in-confusion. As one can clearly see, the tactics are many, and the tactics used are based on the imagination of the sender of the message. Creating the sphere of influence, mounting readiness for physical operations as an additional pressure to sabotage negotiation attempts as needed.

One can have two sets of influencers inside a society. The "wise men" who plan, carry out an executive order, and function towards defined goals. These people are doing the thinking and having a local understanding of the cultural interests of a nation and local regions. There is also a bewildered herd (3), according to Noam Chomsky, that acts as "spectators" but not participating in the action. The "spectators" recommend, lean, and put their weight behind a cause that is in need of public support. They may be members of unions or organizations, and they have the public respect and power of recommendation to say, "let us support this specific person as our leader," or, "I recommend we support this specific action vital to our national interests." In the modern world this can be defined as lobbying, but with a direct or indirect connection to a larger planned mass persuasion for a cause, for example a membership in an organization such as trade pact, military pact, or membership of a union. In the music business these people would be fans and die-hard groupies who also lend their body for a better cause, as long as they get to be in close encounters with their admired fandom. All that, for approval and influence for respect in the eyes of fellow fans towards a group or an individual, such as the vocalist.

Most people use their emotions or simple impulse for guidance, while some have the ability to see through matters, events, hysteria, and fabricated truths. The ones who have the rationality to create the needed illusions and a story behind them can usually also create simplified matters and hyperbole. Presidential campaigns in the United States often have these themes built into them, but as they last for nearly two years, voters often lack interest during the course of the campaign and pick a candidate that has a simple message, has similar values to the voter in visual prospect, and has charisma in terms of representing the dreams and hopes people have, usually involving wealth, well-being, and safety. The power is built with respect and admiration towards an individual, or a small group of individuals supporting the cause for a single contender. Such a cause is easy to relate to and usually easily accepted by the peers of an individual, one's family and friends, and often at least part of a work place.

States build influence within their internal borders to increase nationalism, unity, and integrity. This is essential in many countries to allow the leadership to perform their planned actions in a bigger picture and to enable the ruling party to act according to their desires and plans. Internal influence in a state drives the rulers away from focusing on negatives or problematic issues such as financial or economic views that the nations may experience due to economic downturn, rising unemployment, ecological crisis, or during a state of emergency, martial law, or even an outright declaration of war (4). The influence is built with an overall strategy, split into cycles in varying random lengths, from days to years, with a flexible, pragmatic, scheduled, long haul plan, using various operations and multiple tactics as needed. The progress is made with a clear grand strategy path that follows a fluctuating timeline, which stretches and contracts as a rubber band. Levels of influence vary based on the targeted group of people that need to be influenced. Elites are small in numbers but high in efficacy in the society itself. The high grade influence is built with finance, art, aid, construction deals, and private charter jet etc. In low-grade influence aimed at broad audiences, who are vast in numbers but the expenditure per eye-pair is low, the message is often kept simplified and entertaining; i.e. sports, venues, or reality TV. The toolbox of influence can vary from popular culture items such as TV shows, music, motion picture, books, and articles to language courses, halls and stadiums, and groceries such as taxation of beer and alcohol. Rising efficiency is brought with control of refugee streams, as few countries can manage masses in the hundreds of thousands, creating chaos and an instant downgrade of nation state leadership in the eyes of the voter.

As citizens consume media in a variety of ways, the overall plan of how a nation state intends to run, create, deliver, and distribute the message in a continuous flow. Guide citizens by influence, towards the vision that leaders see in predictive foresight, a decade or two into future. Business people operating in a target country of influence are essential, they are the hands-on people that actually make things work in the field, in a coordinated, efficient fashion. This can be a part of a larger strategy to gain influence with another state. Integration into energy politics, raw material delivery such as crude oil, uranium, electricity, natural gas, or other means of influence such as control of refugee flows. As in any sales process, the bar to accept an offering needs to be low, tempting with instant true benefit. Prices and terms need to be competitive with a special introductory offering, and the message itself, easily understood by masses, a well thought simple solution that solves a short-term problem. At the same time, the elite are lured into the tempting sound of cash and visuals such as art, philanthropic aid, VIP-venues, fashion shows, and luxury items.

Reference:

1. University of Turku, American Study Groups lecture, American History, 2015.
2. University of Turku, American Study Groups lecture, Trauma of an Image, 2015.
3. Chomsky, Noam, Media Control, Second Edition: The Spectacular Achievements of Propaganda.
4. FIIA - Seminar, Media Power in International Politics, Sep 10, 2015, Helsinki
5. The China Journal No. 57, Jan. 2007. Pp. 25-58 by Chicago Journals

3. The Good, The Bad, and The Ugly

We live in new media era, where selfies are taken by soldiers at the altar of war. Posted in real-time to leading Western and Russian social media services, Facebook and VKontakte. Providing a holiday like visuals blended with scout-camp gone bad narratives of war on the Mediterranean coast of Syria. Then revealing the true operations while the official red-hot propaganda machine spreads denial of identical practices on broadcast television. Instant image services, such as Snapchat, and messaging services, such as Twitter, present the atmosphere, look and feel of people, warriors, and victims, timing of attacks, fighter recruitment, the supply or demand for weapons, wins and successes - sometimes on the frontlines spitting bullets with Rambo like gestures. There are even images of self-help like manoeuvres of machine-gun-in-the-air shooting with fighter friends helping hands. Then soldiers taking a break from war operations, while servicing equipment and fishing on the sunny beaches and rivers. All imagery delivered as a non-stop difficult-to-digest fire hose motion image feed. A relentless frame of violence wrapped into customary every-day life with seemingly nothing to worry about, at least that's what we are meant to think while browsing through such imagery.

People watch wars, air disasters, shootings, and poisonings - everything negative, as fear sells - on streaming video websites. An interactive real-life war movie, from their armchairs as hobbyist military evaluators, referees, and educators. They see troops and go-to-war imagery of men loading bombs, and high definition images, still and motion, of them being dropped. Cut and edited as an exciting movie or like an experience to match the video game resembling commercial sales images. Then the imagery is distributed professionally and systematically through media operations. With precision executed tactics, packaged as a well-thought media strategy. Operations fitted into as part of the psychological framework of a nation-state defined frame of threat, the doctrine. Ships and cargo planes transport weapons of all kinds to old Cold War era allies, powered by now middle-aged newcomers of old regimes, and some who have joined new alliances in these times of half-hot-global-war. In today's conflicts, everything is openly available and in the future trillions of sensors of all kinds, flying, static, biological, geographic, nano-level, and beyond will monitor and report everything, leaving nothing secret. The technologic edge the West once had has vanished, removing the effect of tactical leverage. What unites today's powers, the ones thousands of years old and the newcomers in their first decade, is soft power.

Soft power is the way to influence in such a fashion that the set goals are reached without the threshold of a declaration of war and territory can be gained without shooting a single bullet. Cyber attacks steal information, anything from military fighter plane research and development blueprints to military personnel addresses and ranks, as well as the financial information of nearly all citizens who have a bank account, exposing mortgages and savings, to act as a leverage for influence building. This leaves every door open for exploitation. The creation of media influence is a systematic delivery of relentless waves by altering the force and sequence, a constant flux that silently becomes the new normal in the recipient's mind.

The United States' position in the global hierarchy has been unchallenged for two decades. Before that, there was a tight competition with the Soviet Empire - where Reagan's doctrine was to spend the Russians to their ruin, with the freedom to interpret any saying from the Soviet's side to the West's benefit, a plan that worked well enough to win the Cold War. But from 2010 onwards the shape shifting of the world order has begun to change with an increasing tempo. The U.S. position is challenged by a trend of global decision-making split evenly between Beijing, Moscow, Berlin, and Washington. This trend is likely to continue with emphasis towards eastbound. There are also new actors in the game, terrorism is seen as trendy way to fight the United States, causing thousands of wannabe fighters to head from the Western world towards Syria. Northern Africa's failed states of the Sahel area continue to breed easy-to-recruit harvesting for a variety of terrorist organisations. This trend will continue, with a strengthening flow, as the human resource is unlimited in volume. Russia has projected a strong focus on the polar area and will continue efforts to establish even larger areas under its control, also causing the illusionary border of Russia's nuclear submarine fleet to edge closer to the North American shores.

Life is now global with low language barriers to relocate where social connections, work and culture meet. Global citizens are able to travel from one country to another in hours, as there are professions that do not require the life-long placement of a residence. Expanded knowledge and the ability to fluently speak several languages are soon available for more people. Humans on Earth no longer feel tied to a single country but can resettle in their preferred location, which causes a transfer of knowledge, posing a challenge for countries. At the same time masses of refugees and fugitives, illegal immigrants, and infiltrated terrorist, all having similar external appearances, in need of humanitarian help, stress the European Union states with a need to re-evaluate the agreements between countries. This opens up the discussion of agreed ways to handle open movement. Politicians in Brussels oppose any changes, denying the facts and changes of the world status, holding on to their decisions and local regional votes for their personal good, with support delivered through local media.

All relations and facts reflect the current status; there are millions of moving variables at any given time in a society or corporation, movement of citizens and customers towards socially approved ways to function. The tempo of global events increase and reaction times to competitor operations shorten, with predictive and prescriptive systems becoming essential pieces of information creation for constant market simulation.

The technological advance was created through America's vast pool of universities, which created and recruited high talent, nation state leaders and research know-how. The edge in technology, research, and development has shortened due to mass scale production globally. Systematic stealing of company secrets and blueprint from the design tables of Boeing, Northrop-Grumman, and Martin Marietta, to name a few, have caused the leading position to first narrow and then disappear, as state run competitors from China are using any means possible to vaporise the technological lead by ruthless poaching. The systematic way in which China and Russia have stolen U.S. personal, bank, finance, tax, sports, and defence information have reached all dimensions in society. This has not been limited to credit card information, as in the Target incident that effected tens of millions of people, but also dating services in order to humiliate and internally fracture the mental state of individuals in government organisations, bank account information, as in the J.P. Morgan incident that affected 70 million people, and the Ashley Madison hack of 37 million accounts, including 15,000 U.S. military personnel, are just a small piece of the total number of hacks made (1). Chinese hackers are often either directly connected to the People's Liberation Army or they are built-to-order hacks, ordered by state actors. Over 4 million government personnel files were poached, including social security numbers, in 2015. Before that, the Internal Revenue Service exposed over 100,000 tax records, information that was hacked by groups close to the Kremlin. Combining all that stolen information creates a relation network that present people of a country in a matrix where an analyst of average skill can extract groups of people; those who have high income or low income, lots of kids or no kids, two cars, three or more, a mortgage over a half a million, employed by the government or a specific corporation, and if their marriage is likely on the brink of collapse. Medium power, with stolen data through cybercrime, combined with soft power, propaganda for influence, create an environment that is efficient to fight today's silent wars. Such news may be interesting to watch, at times, from one's living room, as long as it is not your city, or the elevator you are in, that ends up totally blind for days due to a cyber attack on the electrical network.

For U.S. and European businesses and corporations, it is high time to enact measures and the ability to block intrusive attempts. In the U.S. the volume of accounts in data hacks now reach nearly all of citizens. All of them in multiple dimensions reaching personal finances, connections, friends, lovers, military rank and branch, work tasks, and personal liabilities. The intelligence operatives in China and Russia must be thrilled with how they can see through the society in nearly every way imaginable depending on their need, who knows who, who to influence, who to bribe, and so on.

Because of these and related events, facts, and times - the United States no longer holds a central place in the world and is unable to meet expectations of companies and its citizens. Allies are looking around for partners either to have a plan B or to team up with other countries in similar situations, even former adversaries. In earlier times vanishing power was transferred to emerging powers but this may not be the case anymore. The past hegemony of a single actuator is spread throughout the world. The number of aircraft carriers may still have some effect, but in a digitized world information is the oil, and knowledge is the gasoline of everyday decision-making. The global digital life, virtualized environments, and connections beyond political and geographic lines change the former model of geographic blocks. Global relations of interdependencies cause complex, fast changing environments to understand the status of matters. Combined future scenarios and recommendations create *prescriptive foresight* (4). Even further, one needs to see beyond the look-a-like facilitators switching from soft to hard to medium power. When looking at the world, and the models of hybrid warfare, nearly every country is in an asymmetric war, with a single or multiple parties. In some cases, there are multiple adversaries in a single state. It is likely that more nations slide into a variety of hybrid wars with non-human casualties, as economic and virtual damages appear over a longer time frame than instant air strikes. The United States is losing its grip of influence, as the nation is jammed in administrative stagnation, transferring taxpayer monies to shareholders with over budgeted defence contracts that lack true competition due to over merged corporate markets. Without placing investment bets on new outcomes and scenarios, the past power diminishes, causing the erosion of global hegemony with an ever-faster pace.

In the United States, the leader is the engine and concerned people the fuel. The American middle class feels they have been betrayed by their inept administration leadership. In Russia, the leader is a demagogue and the engine, and hysteria among people the fuel. Putin's Russia seeks nations' and their people's respect by force and threats, through military might being developed into the 2020s'.

Donald Trump's vision of success is based on the promise of wealth and victory with tit for tat of the ruling elite. With a return of America as the leader of the free world. While Putin seeks to establish a series of naval and airbases in the Mediterranean Sea, Baltic States, and Northern Arctic Sea, leaving the South China Sea and parts of the Pacific Ocean for China. Airbases with heavy paved runways able to carry long-range bomber squadrons have already been built on Spratly Islands, Johnston Atolls, and the vicinity and equipped with missile bases of various sorts (5). Trump handles matters through trade and economics, but he is also ready to declare war on ISIS and send the Army, Navy, and Air Force to take the areas that have oil and gas from the criminal regimes. A strong leader demands a bold strategy, but may well be softened when the realism of daily politics come into play after their inauguration.

The potential can be harnessed by the guidance and direction of an assertive leader. Obama started out well in his first term, but eroded during the second term to a tug-of-war with Capitol Hill. An innovative mindset blended with a relentless will and grit allowed the U.S. to transform itself from the early 20th century local power to the Western power of the victorious Second World War. Reagan's strong commitment, decisive maneuvers, and offensive strategy took down the Soviet Union, with operations in the media and popular music arena. After a decade of hegemony, the United States was caught with their pants down, the Twin Towers were hit in September 2001 and this intertwined the nation in two wars in Iraq and Afghanistan. The 9/11 attacks shocked the nation and created a visual trauma of tragedy. These still images have since been repeatedly presented in global media. This was comparable to the attack on Pearl Harbor that brought the U.S. into the Second World War.

Osama bin-Laden created a global brand of himself and the group he presented in 30 minutes on a clear morning, but paid the highest price a decade later. While al-Qaeda was old fashioned in its mind-set, their operations were successful. However, they did not see the amplifying capacity of social media to relay their message globally. ISIS understood this and created a strategy of *digihad*. A manufactured visual lure, the Call of Jihad (6), is presented with movie and video game like visuals. Social media is used to echo the terroristic rhetoric on Facebook, then real-time execution orders are distributed on Twitter, and documentation of achievements is presented on YouTube. This set of messaging methods took down governments in Tunis, Libya, and Egypt. ISIS influences western teenagers with visual built-to-order truths that act as a façade for a devious message to turn against their civilizations. A visual glamour covered terroristic message is easy to distribute to millions of people, to catch the potential ones who feel distanced from western societies, buying into the faux success of terror. The strong visuals combined with a pop idol like leadership creates a virtual reality, an easy sell of radical Islam to people in their teens. It is depicted as glamour, an easy life at the pool, fighting the imagined adversary of the West. A message distributed by western media. In reality the newcomers end up in mine fields and frontline fighting that takes a hard toll on the men. Ladies are forced to marry get pregnant. Even younger fighters, 8 to 12 year-olds end up fighting according to ISIS leadership. The vision of fandom, the pop star like imagery, a cool life, and driving a Lamborghini does not end up quite as planned. The young recruited people do not see the facts, but an illusion portrayed for them on the web.

Donald Trump uses the methods that got Ronald Reagan elected, bluntness and even amusement, but in a more Americanized way of these times. Both of them presented as unconventional outsiders. The American forgotten middle class wanted their revenge towards the elite of Washington. They did not receive their promised share of the family dream, a house with a two-car garage, a pool, and friends at a barbecue party, the blissful life. Instead they got an average of $5,000 of funds at the average age of 34 (7). They are the fed-up crowd, the optimal supporters for a strong leader. Some say this is a populist theme, as others hail for new hope. Trump's wealth makes him unstoppable; he has a clear and strong message, something that is easy for listeners to "buy into". At the same time other parties, such as China and Russia, are eagerly looking for which section of the former U.S. power can be annexed. The power vacuum that an ailing America leaves behind is quickly filled in with Chinese influence in Africa and South-East Asia, and Russian influence with dividing tactics in Europe. This trend escalates with Russia and China stealing all they can get their hands on; U.S. and EU trade secrets, corporate research and development, and insurance, payment, tax, and financial information ruthlessly through cyberwar fare. The aligning world views of the Russian conservatism, and the U.S. heartland conservative-biblical views do not overlap but are slightly closer than residents realize - the fearful West and the hysteric East.

The European Union is incapable operating on the world stage as a single entity. The Western image of an enemy is painted towards Russia and its allies. The West is a drifting empire, as the Soviet Empire once was, with the need of clear story and path forward. The large-scale power play projects being built by ISIS, supported by Islamic allies with painted images of an enemy. Russia operates with vengeance to humiliate the United States and China with its own global hegemony project to gain their share of the planet. The West needs a strong leader to ensure stability and balance in the world. Otherwise the stability is lost, which creates a world disorder and anarchy that no one in the West or Asia wants to see or experience. Russia will gladly accept the victim's role, this ensures a powerful information strike to slice Europe and divide created alliances. One cannot know whether Russian leaders may be holding back the generals and security officials that would advance to hit back for revenge for humiliation suffered in early 1990's.

If the West wants to stay intact, it needs to take bold steps to regain the technologic edge it had in 1980's. It must agree on spending at the state level to turn the budget deficit into a surplus, ensure unity as a whole, or accept an alternative route, the U.S. dollar is removed from the world stage, our grandkids speak Mandarin Chinese and study Russian as their first and Arabic as second language. The United Nations may still exist in New York, Geneva, and Vienna, but do leaders listen to the UN out of courtesy? While they read Twitter messages of speeches and rumors, they project power remotely to their local voter precinct.

Reference:

1. http://www.informationisbeautiful.net/visualizations/worlds-biggest-data-breaches-hacks/
2. http://www.fool.com/personal-finance/taxes/2015/05/31/the-terrifying-method-hackers-used-to-steal-nearly.aspx
3. Russia: 7-year cyberwar against Nato, EU and US by Kremlin-sponsored hackers – The Dukes exposed, September 17, 2015
4. Forthcast.com future modeling.
5. The Economist
6. Daily Mail, 3rd. February 2015
7. http://www.gobankingrates.com/savings-account/62-percent-americans-under-1000-savings-survey-finds/
8. Leino, Sami, Startup Africa, Chapter: Terrorism.

SAMI LEINO

Media Crisis Recovery

This is how tamper proof seals became the industry standard for medicine products - and a prominent medical company turned the tide of 31 million pills, which was about to sink them, indefinitely.

It was late evening on September 30th 1982, when Adam Janus, 27, was having chest pain. Nothing special at first, but he felt a more severe spike in his chest and decided to take a Tylenol pill. He collapsed. The drug had become a market leader in the United States during the 1970s and well known throughout the country. After taking the pill Adam died. When his brother and sister arrived at his house they were terrified, and took pills themselves, with identical consequences (2). Somewhere in the distribution and the packaging line, someone had switched the capsules with cyanide capsules, looking identical to the original ones. No one could see outright the deadly force in them. Then four other people died after taking the pill, totaling seven in all. Soon, police patrol cars were driving around Chicago and advising people not to take any of the aforementioned pills. All of them would be recollected and purchased by McNeil, the manufacturer of Tylenol. People became hysteric and all of the pills were removed from the shelves of retailers. While watching the news we felt a bit uncomfortable. Halloween was only couple weeks away and kids in our area, as well as around the United States, were told to be careful regarding the candy they received. No candy should be eaten until checked by parents. Eventually copycat incidents occurred, such as needles in candy bars, which terrified Halloween weekend that year (2).

McNeil offices first though it was a hoax. At parent company Johnson & Johnson headquarters in New Brunswick, New Jersey, the Chairman and the President were having a meeting. They had done well in the economic recession. A member of the executive committee stormed in and informed everyone that there had been poisonings in Chicago with Tylenol. The company went through a series of shocks, and a three-phase recovery process; it tried to understand what happened, it then tried to contain and assess the damage, and in the third phase get back into the market. An attempt that everyone knew would take years, if ever. The story was all over the news, the company received calls not only from the US but from Europe as well. Management did their best to screen out location of purchases, causes of deaths, lot numbers of poisoned bottles, dates of manufacturing, and the route of distribution. The trail lead to steel machines in the state of Washington that spew out pills at the rate of over 35,000 pills per hour (1). They decided to push all the information out to the public as openly as possible to minimize further damages. Later during a company-destroying day, the management learned that there was cyanide used in quality assurance for purity testing of the materials in the manufacturing process. The back and forth hassle made the company look even even worse hour by hour, but honest and open communication helped the organization get back on its feet.

The Tylenol brand suffered enormous losses in the eyes of consumers, but the company was determined to have the product back on shelves. Regardless of how hard the press would whip them, the one hundred million dollars spent on the recall alone would only be a starting point, and a start from square one. The company executives pledged that regardless of what consumer research gave as reports, the market surveys present attitudes not behaviour. Therefore, the best way to know what people really thought was to put the product back on shelves as soon as possible - let them vote with their wallets but this time in a fixed product format. The solution was an unbreakable bottle and sealing that cannot be opened and then closed again without the user being fully aware. Not just visually but also by feel of hand. Once opened, the bottle felt as if it were broken with a sharp plastic edge on the seal itself (2).

In a media disaster such as this, timing was essential. This was psychological warfare. Having the product back too soon meant hysteria hadn't subsided. The product would re-brand itself with a stay-away image. Difficult if not impossible to wear off from the brand. Naturally, competitors received an unforeseen opportunity to gain market share. So it was important not to wait too long to restart building market share from zero. The message was of the utmost importance, both to doctors and pharmacists. A discrete simplified message; there was a crime committed, and we are sorry, but in response, we have invented packaging that will help prevent anyone from doing such atrocities again. The company offered a free alternative version of the product and coupons to purchase more of the same at a considerable discount. At the same time, preparations for a fierce comeback were being prepared. Four weeks after the fatal incidents, the company's chief operation officer mobilized 2,259 sales people to approach medical personnel, to work their way up from their crashed market share of seven percent, just as they did when they started over two decades earlier. After a year they were back at nearly the same levels, at the pre-crisis level of 37% market share, with the mantra, first the people, then the product (1).

The subsidiary McNeil, the company manufacturing Tylenol, eventually survived. They fought their way out of the fatal situation, which drove down Johnson & Johnson's annual results by over 30% in a media debacle that could have cost the whole company to go under (3). This event created the gold standard of crisis management. And the triple seal tamper resistant packaging became the norm after the events of that late September evening of 1982.

Reference:
1. Time by Dan Fletcher Monday, Feb. 09, 2009
http://content.time.com/time/nation/article/0,8599,1878063,00.html
2. Authors personal recollection of events.
3. Wikipedia, Tylenol Murders.

Media is what it is - But what is it?

News is an information burst, caused by a sudden event, reaction to new or past activity, or the revelation of hidden story. News is distributed on broadcast television, newspapers, blogs, and websites, published and amplified by social media. News anchors present the brand of the news, the credibility spearhead of information. Future news anchors may rise from the audience that are elected by the viewers themselves. In the 2020's news could be seen as above, but created by a mash up of news anchors, reporters, broadcast companies, individuals, and social media as relayed message that echoes in short bursts recreating itself constantly until the item is pushed aside by the next item.

News comes and goes, some of us are starting to evade the constant negative news of wars and bombings. People will seclude and protect themselves and their families from the visual violence of the news. News is an information flow of various levels and sectors, presented by a variety of content types. Controlling the news is difficult. Media control is a challenge. Constant flow of the truth, semi-truth, and distorted messages, even lies, are difficult for viewer to extract and find the true meaning of a message. A message in Twitter service may catch people's eyes at different times of the day, and as we have 40 times zones in the world as some countries have half an hour and even 15-minute zones. This causes waves of acceptance or repentance of such news. Each time when a new set of people start their commute to work they turn on their screens, reading and watching, experiencing the escalating coarsening language, as a new wave of people review the earlier comments of the people before them. The negative words pile on top of each other creating exponential news negatives, sometimes also positives, quickly destroying an individual or corporate brand. "So what," some can say, "does news really affect my life out there running or cycling?" It does not directly, but indirectly many of us feel that a person isn't even alive if not connected to social media at all time. Social media is the reflection of an individual, the echo of ideas and thoughts of how one reacts to news items being thrown at them from omnipresence of information sphere, consisting of gossip, fact, say, opinion, or any mash-up of the previous. The challenge in future times is to clarify the border of fact and community agreed set of beliefs. A well verified set of facts that the majority of us in society believe in becomes fact, and further on knowledge. A well agreed bunch of gossip, stirred and colored with imagination, agreed on by the masses in social media, becomes social knowledge. Not exactly a fact in the traditional sense, but a fact for those millions who believe in the message of social media more than the violence saturated constant flow of death from major news channels.

As a story develops it changes the normality of the story environment, escalating, increasing, or decreasing its meaning in the eyes of the recipient, viewer, and listener. Constant presentation of violence numbs the viewer. Constant negative news of specific region places a negative. When such messages saturate the medias it becomes challenging for anyone to see and understand the new level of normality of the content and message itself. The reality of news content itself varies and blurs as messages are presented in an identical framework, for example in social media. The source of the news is essential to verify its credibility. News agencies rely on each other, while individuals want to experience their version of the non-fact based world, colliding with real and surreal worlds of information. Traditional media rebroadcasts the information burst first presented in social media as the primary source of the news, trailing the information flow, instead of taking the lead. This causes the traditional premium brand broadcast media to come second to the community-powered media's stir of news. Traditional media can counter this trend by inserting in-depth knowledge to their broadcast keeping the respectability or credibility among their viewers.

Good Muslim - Evil Muslim

In the TV series Homeland, Carrie (Claire Danes), a.k.a Drone Queen, is a CIA chief of intelligence operator. She spends a night with Aayan, a Muslim college kid in Lahore Pakistan who she is trying to seduce information from. Aayan is the only survivor of a drone strike gone bad that killed everyone else at a wedding. Aayan was able to submit video shots of what and how it happened to YouTube. He becomes wanted by the local security service, the ISI. Carrie and Aayan get along well, even though Carrie has a broader picture in mind, to have the young medical student lead US intelligence to the nest of the chief terrorist, a bomb maker. She plays a game with Aayan, whose uncle is the chief terrorist. Carrie has a sincere intention to send the medical student to study at the Royal Medical School in London, but events take a turn for worse, at least for Carrie's plan: The uncle pulls a gun and shoots Aayan outright, after thanking him for bringing medical supplies for his kidney disease. The chief terrorist receives the evil Muslim hat in the visual scenery of the story and Aayan is the victim, a harmless and lamblike 20-something who becomes the good Muslim for the viewer.

The TV series presents a contradictory two-way street of the Muslim world - not being all-out belligerent towards the United States, as media has mostly presented since the 9/11 terrorist attacks - but also having humane aspects. The US media keeps the victimization scar open and enables the viciousness of Muslims as needed for US interests; political or economic, defense or offense. While the viciousness of Muslims has been maintained in the US media since 9/11/2001. There has also been viewer discretion being too much against Muslims for some series. A good Muslim theme has been implemented into the script to have the balance that viewers crave. In fact, ratings and viewer figures had risen once the polarization had been added to motion pictures (1). In the end, there is a hero written into the script, a hero that either saves the West, the US, or at least gives a determined push towards western values.

Little Mosque on The Prairie (2), a Canadian production sitcom, was an extreme of this media space, taking the discussion and commentary to ridicule and defaming 9/11 victims. The sitcom played with the idea of touching a sacred classic TV series of pilgrims travelling to the west in the 1800's, turned into a self-mockery of Muslim cultural values. Life of the family faces challenges of modern day Muslims and the western perceptions of them. The sitcom ran for six seasons and was fairly popular, with a variety of ratings and interpretations on what is appropriate and what can be publicly judged, with or without being stamped as a bigoted or racist. In the commentary of the series, viewers use the term racist, sometimes not even reading or viewing the content or knowing what the phrase actually means. United States is a divided country in terms of races and their cultures. Muslims are secluded into their slot in the media structure, similar in perspective to other viewers.

Reference:

1. University of Turku American Study Group lectures, Trauma of an image, Jan-Mar 2015.
2. TV Series Little Mosque on The Prairie, CBC Television Co., Ltd, 2006-2012.

Who's Truth?

The Russian run news channel RT interviews so-to-say "news experts" who present their specialist opinion to enhance, add credibility, and provide an in-depth knowledge of a news story. Sometimes these "professionals" have been presented with made up pen names, to disseminate counter information to likes of BBC, CNN, and Al-Jazeera. News channels compete with message and aim to drive their agenda towards an agreed worldview that matches and fits the government agreed agenda. The media broadcasts intend to saturate the world with information that presents their view of the world. The coverage by these major channels is saturating most news that happens in the world. Budgets for these giants are enormous with the BBC and RT ranging $200-400 million dollar annually. All four media giants provide a global narrative of world in their government's favor. According to comScore and Statista.com, RT is strong with on demand television outside Anglo-Saxon countries, but lags in the broadcast market share. In the United States, CNN leads with 17% percent of people preferring the channel as their primary news source. 58% of people find the content of CNN credible. BBC is preferred by 71% of viewers in the U.K. and globally the figure hovers around 76 million weekly viewers. Al-Jazeera is popular in the Middle East with a audience potential of over 300 million viewers, currently claiming over 40 online million viewers. Among these four channels the market shares of online viewers are roughly BBC 40%, RT and Al-Jazeera both at slightly less than a 25%, and CNN at 15%. Other major news providers are Deutsche Welle, France 24, Al Arabiya, Euronews, Sky News, MSNBC, NDTV India, CCTV China, and NHK World Japan.

Reference:
comScore, CNN, BBC, Al-Jazeera, RT, October – November, 2015
Wikipedia, Broadcast media

Trauma of an Image

After the 2015 Metrojet Airbus charter flight bombing in Sinai and the November Paris massacre of the same year, both operated by the terrorist group ISIS and its factions. Presidents Francois Hollande and Vladimir Putin had similar views on their mindset and mental landscape - determination, perseverance, and a silent rage for revenge for killing their nationals but also humiliating them as leaders. Hollande also visited Washington at the same time. In world politics, there is consensus only when there is a greater force, such as global terrorism, to connect the global powers for cooperation.

Repercussions of crimes against humanity often carry out a great public message of, "We are at war!" to enforce a positive view and approval for every leader who participates in such a front, but quite often the news decay factor kicks in after some weeks and months, depending on the severity of the event, and the outcome starts to degrade unless it is emphasized by the regional and global media as a productized package. With still and motion imagery and strong terminology, the repetition of the media ensures that audiences remember the simplified message. These messages can then be disseminated in 10-30 second impulses to bolster the borderless war against terrorism. Statesmen perform pinpoint messaging to the masses, in a straightforward way, to condemn opponents and justify their actions on the world media stage.

9/11 and Cultural Trauma

Images of the economic and defence symbols of power; the Pentagon, the World Trade Center towers, the Capitol, and the White House were either hit or were under imminent threat, resembling visual imagery of a trauma, that is still healing. The media has branded each state and city. New York equals finance, San Francisco and the Bay Area is technology, Los Angeles is entertainment, the Midwest mainly agriculture but also oil and gas production, Florida for retirement, and Washington D.C. stands as the symbol of power.

When the terrorists, all Muslim, mostly originating from, and all funded by, Saudi-Arabia, accessed the US through Germany and Canada, being trained to take-off but not land in Florida, hit the WTC towers, the Pentagon created a trauma of a memory for people in the United States, and also for many in Europe. Western values peace and harmony were attacked. When the towers were hit, the first news story was about a small plane that had hit a WTC tower in New York. It felt like a movie for viewers to see the WTC attacks on live television, watching CNBC after the first plane had hit the north tower and seeing live how the second plane hit the south tower, and eventually both towers collapsing, it felt surreal, effects and reality mixed into disaster movie morning news.

First came CNN, cutting straight out from whatever they were airing, with live picture from their newsroom. It was a far away view but with some zoom the people waving clothes from towers could well be seen. Then came FOX displaying the identical view of the towers from New Jersey, ABC commenting from closer range in Downtown Manhattan, and eventually CBS, after commercials finished, starting to display what was available on feed from CNN.

The media flow, in the morning hours of September 9th created a cultural visual trauma. It undermined the collective identity, how people felt about the West and especially the United States. This was an *invasive media event* that overwhelmed everyone watching the news globally, similar to a disaster motion picture but indecipherable and surreal in human understanding. Most people could not understand what was happening, reacting in chilling emotive defence. Some cried, some raged, and some were in shock. People in hotels in Manhattan had an urge, at about the same time, to exit the hotel rooms and the hallways, quickly striding to the nearest open area such as Central Park. A human survival instinct drove everyone present without full control of one's mind urging for an answer "why head to an open space?" The primary need for everyone is safety and at that moment no one felt safe. This was the intent of al-Qaeda, the terrorist organization that carried out the operation, masterminded by Usama Bin-Laden.

The giant of a nation was vulnerable, will we recover, and can our administration keep us safe? These were the thoughts of the masses as people cried on the news videos reflecting the collective shock, then reflecting to endless discussions, TV series, adverts, motion pictures, even song lyrics. Throughout society every class and every location processed the consequences.

Storytelling changed. Caring and unity became top-level topics. Relevancy of real-time media became a necessity. Content needed to be on-demand rather than delivered at a specific time. Listening to the voices of the victims both on the news and through phones on the hi-jacked, weaponized plane, gripped everyone and forced them to interpret the events as if they were a part of them. Everyone was forced to go through the process on a first hand basis.

What follows is a call made to my friend in Dallas seconds after the first plane hit, early morning on 9/11/2001:
I had a phone line open some seconds after the 9/11 event with my colleague in Dallas, Texas. Right after the collapse of the twin towers, when the phone lines still worked, 15 minutes afterwards and the transatlantic lines were jammed for days due to capacity limitations and worries about security issues. I asked my friend about the situation and his opinion about the towers as we both felt there could be a way to rebuild them, as I knew he was an architect. "At least they have to cut down the towers, if not dismantle them wholly and then rebuild," was his first comment. I felt disappointed, as my wife and I had just visited the entrance level some months before but decided to see the sights in the Empire State Building instead due to long lines at the South Tower of the WTC. He continued, "I wonder what their reaction will

be. I doubt it will be anything small." Once the first tower tumbled down, the world as we saw it changed forever. U.S. intelligence had all the information to prevent the event from happening but the facts were on different tables, in separate systems, causing the big picture to have more holes than cheese.

Reference:
1. The Cultural Sociology of Political Assassination: Ron Eyerman
2. University of Turku lectures, Trauma of an image, January – March 2015.

Media building on 9/11/2001

When the 9/11/2001 attacks happened, a trauma was created by visualizing the suffering of people. This trauma was created by photos and video close-ups of shocked countrymen. It was then maintained systematically, in the state of "we will never forget," by using considerable prime time to display images of trauma, not only of American victims, but the West in general. The same media play endured after the London attacks on 7/11/2005 and the Madrid train attacks in 2004. Media uses the live TV time and repetitions that create and then maintain the trauma in systematic fashion. The trauma takes a moment from people's everyday lives, without a cause, and summarizes suffering to define its size and volume, repetitions and occurrence, fading year by year. All this makes Americans victims, victimizing the nation, along with the United Kingdom, France, Germany, Spain, and the West in general. Everyone seeing the news images becomes a victim themselves, whether they were present at Ground Zero or not. These actions also bring out the internal heroic actions in people and bring continuance to fight the insurgents.

These major media events changed values in society. First by issuing total support for presidents, monarchies, and governments, and then settling in harmony with the day-to-day life. Further, such activity reflects by allowing support for all law enforcement actions, also causing freedom of interpretation of the ethical use of interrogation. During the third phase, the nation awakens, and starts to question the ways to fight the war. As knowledge spreads in society, people desire to take justice into their own hands.

This all delivers power and influence, and adjusts values of society at the personal and national level. In the case of 9/11, this first became American heroism, then spread into Spain, the United Kingdom, France, and onwards to Europe and the Far East. All this modifies perspectives and allows acceptance for hard measures for some time. There is debate, and vows to never forget. When time decay kicks in the minds of the global audiences' people go back to their daily lives and eventually new crises and events rise above the noise. For participants suffering the loss of a close family member or a colleague, the memory never fades, it carries forward for generations to come. The media, from time to time, maintains the trauma nationwide and allows the administration to plan, act, and benefit with the backing of the earlier trauma. A major media event is an enabler for government action and the nation's future political plans and internal decisions.

After the September 11, 2001 terrorist attacks on the World Trade Center the media started to package and productize the event based on non-related facts, with emotional news broadcasting, where interviews were conducted with people in tears, who could barely speak or tell their stories. This created a visual drama concurrently with the information flow, and then created victims and heroes, firemen, police and medical units. Journalism of these events became similar despite the broadcaster. We present emotion with a sentimental sadness and empathy, through shocking images of victims, which enforces a heroic story and visual legacy. The media presented an external threat, which cumulated in a wave of hate that attacked the United States, resulting in global revenue for American ideology. 9/11 events were also an export event of American unity, but with a enormous cost of nearly 3000 lives.

During the Vietnam War, support of the people was critical. Whereas during the aftermath of 9/11 the new era of terrorist hunts presented a reflection, with broad rights granted by politicians to intelligence. The U.S. victimized itself, establishing a global right to revenge with a vengeance. Also the entertainment machine of Hollywood got interested, and soon the villains and heroes switched places between various security organizations. This actually started some years before the 9/11 attacks in 1998. In that year Dan Brown, in his book Digital Fortress, writes about a finale where the breaking of a password is in the center of the plot. The password turns out to be a single, alphanumeric character, hardly a credible mode of security by any means.

The TV series 24 (1), from the year 2001 onwards, presented a favorable view, as the CIA, FBI, and some sort of rough counter-terrorist unit together. The series started sometime after the 9/11 WTC terrorist attacks, pledging national security for the United States. New media age of safety took over television, presented by Jack Bauer, the top counter terrorist detective-assassin-agent. At the same time presenting a caring family man who tries to keep up with his struggling family life while protecting the country. All this presents a mental immersion and hope that a government is able to protect its citizens who believe in its core values; liberty, justice, individualism, equality, and happiness. But at the same time noticing that a violation in one's privacy in a modern western society is a mere detail. The safety that a society provides comes with the cost of privacy. Either there is all the privacy one desires with successful terrorist attacks, or there is some privacy but terrorism fails most of the time. Therefore, government succeeds in its mission to provide and produce a reasonable framework for its citizens to live their lives. This is a balance of privacy and safety, society cannot have both. There needs to be a ratio of fairness that is reasonable for most citizens, according to the rules of democracy.

Individual rights in modern society are the opposite of totalitarianism, autocracy, and mass processing security systems. These causes and risks compete in the minds of citizens, switching places depending on the occurrence of terrorist events. China and Russia have enhanced their capabilities in "everything information," however at the same time, geographically secured corporate operators such as Google have state-of-the-art security systems that are superior in preventing unauthorized access to its customer emails and files for both private and corporate customers. Global corporations put their full weight behind security that acts as a spearhead for their brand. The fear factor is a key part of today's message delivered by the media in most countries, as this negativity kills creativity, one should carefully evaluate the amount of front page news to digest as a counter weight to successful thoughts and business itself, as negativity builds nothing but low energy in one's professional performance. Our daily lives are filled with constant media-flow, which tends to legitimize surveillance to enforce our security, but at the same time endangering the belief in our society of norms and laws through ultimate information gathering. The media is used to paint a picture that is needed to justify the wars in Iraq and Afghanistan.

The TV series Madam Secretary (2) presents a political drama flavored for all audiences during the prime time hours for CBS. The narrative characterizes Elisabeth Adam McCord, played by Téa Leoni, as the U.S. secretary of state, as humane and modest, but tough as needed, a person who prefers soft power methods instead of military action. The series draws wise maneuvers and wit. Without apoplectic aggression that viewers globally have been used to seeing in multiple media fought wars, from the 1990's and 2000's.

"There is plenty of room in the world for mediocre men, but there is no room for mediocre women" - Madeleine Albright, in the TV series Madam Secretary, episode 2, season 2. (2)

The series presents scuffles played in the backrooms of the Pentagon. Between chosen strategy and the surrounding psychological threat defines towards an adversary as to exploit opportunities with medium power or to calm the situation. The series also plays around the narrative of rebels in Taliban controlled areas somewhere in or around Afghanistan. Another similar TV series is State of Affairs, a thriller drama about an ex-CIA officer taken from the field to assist the U.S. president as the daily briefer, also presenting the lead role as a successful and strong woman of the 2010's, played by Katherine Heigl (3).

The media operates messages and narratives, the discourse of politics and mass persuasion in our societies. From democracies to autocracies and Africapitalism to the Chinese single party model, it depends on who is asking and who has the right to define what is a justified and safe society. This differs for each country in the world, and how it is achieved. George Bush won a second term, but he would not have won a hypothetical third as there weren't weapons of mass destruction in Iraq and the decay of time factor started to build with people forgetting parts of 9/11 traumas and focusing on their day-to-day problems, such as unemployment, house prices, and mortgage rates. The critique towards Bush increased as time went by and the alternative media, smartphones with YouTube, and social networks took over the media field with an increased criticality towards earlier decisions. The media field changed radically from 2001 to 2011, as there were over 50,000 new blogs being set up some for days after 9/11 attacks, but a decade after the communication had gone further for individuals to create the news, flavored with their personal opinion.

The voices in media started to multiply into various voices on how much the U.S. created violence in far-away countries, child and civilian casualties of war, and the prison camp of Guantanamo, all started to flow through YouTube, democratizing media dissemination and adding a level of difficulty in controlling the media flow. The major media flow demanded ethics and values. All this adds fear, which causes more problems running a nation or a media department of a corporation.

The American viewpoint can be myopic, on CNN a vision of a world where everyone watching wants and thinks the same things Americans want, eventually with aligned values. That is the intention of the pro-American message in the narrative of the channel. Whereas BBC presents a British civilized society, which understands and welcomes people of various backgrounds, but only with willingness to honor British values. This same reverberation echoes in the discourse of most western news channels, such as France24, Sky News, and Deutsche Welle. However, these broadcast stories are unable to connect to terroristic minds and make an impact on the adversarial audiences. Terroristic propaganda is not only about competing for hearts and minds, it is about rising above the blandness of general media and the noise of social media, being a game of 'who dares wins'.

Western societies do not approve security by any means. Amended privacy, the intent to secure anything by any means, approaches totalitarian society. The intent of security efforts by any means, focus, and targets; judges, politicians, critics, intellectuals, citizens, and corporations, define the direction where society as whole is headed. The privacy of citizens is being taken as a hostage of collateral damage, when drawing the line between security and collateral privacy.

Reference:
1. TV Series 24
2. TV Series Madam Secretary
3. TV Series State of Affairs, Rotten Tomatoes
4. Järvinen Petteri, NSA - Näin Meitä Seurataan, 2014, p. 38-40.

4. Smart Power

Nation State Brand

"Power is like weather, everyone depends on it, and talks about it, but few understand it." Joseph S. Nye

Leaders, politicians, and analysts do their best to evaluate power, to predict its change in relationships and benefit from allies or vacuums to gain more influence. Power is like love, fun to experience but difficult to measure or control. Power is the outcome one wants. To end up where or how you want to be, you can coerce with threats, induce with a contribution, or cooperate with others who want the same target as you do.

In order to understand power change, and to measure it, we have to know others' preferences. Coercive power lasts only as long as the opponents, who power is projected to, has an alternative as a choice, environment, or status. Power projection through sticks and carrots may be useful, but oftentimes you receive the same results with soft power. Power is relative to the relationship connection between its holder and servant, and sometimes the outcome is received without affecting behaviour without forced command. If one believes in the objectives of the power holder, and the message sender holds a credible appearance, then one listens to such as a message. In social media, this would be accomplished by "Following" the message sender, for example on Twitter or LinkedIn.

Smart Power is adapting to external challenges, with predefined sets of solutions (1). Guidance, persuasion, and diplomacy are a mix of soft power and related methods. Avoiding the use of power in the traditional means, such as armed conflicts, is essential to save resources. Methods of smart power consist of adaptability and responding to each situation with a tailored solution. The content of the crisis does not automate a trigger of predefined consequences. Rather it gathers up a group of specialists from various sectors in the society, who define the best solution, a customised set of procedures (1). The procedures then define methods to be used for a specific crisis. Smart Power is post-modernist power, where the end result is intended to be achieved without sanctions and trade barriers. The arts and culture are an efficient and long-term method of influence, often with a fixed outpost, permanent or at least lasting for years. The Louvre and Guggenheim museums represent western smart power and the expansion of western interpretation of history.

Information is power and distributing information is challenging due to constant media noise. Good propaganda is no propaganda at all, as the recipient doesn't notice it. It is about building near-abroad or far-abroad influence by posing the desired message in a positive light towards specific targets. Those targets may be, or may have been, adversarial, bound to another military ally, economic block, or political camp. Since today's world is interconnected it is worthwhile to plan strategic models that have a vast array of tactical tools. This is full-spectrum warfare, consisting of political power, the equation of control of territory, information, political influence and activities, strategic resources and diplomatic discussions. It is about presenting nations and citizens in a tempting or rejecting the model. Nation that is presented positive or negative perspective. Building soft power between nation-states, or within an industry, is created in the long term over multiple years, or even decades.

The build-up of soft power is set of variety information paths, each of them having a separate time cycle. Influence through the quick lanes causes swift reactions in the targeted group of people. A medium presentation of information has a wide variety of influence build-up and reaction. Slow, long-term influence takes years, or decades, to build-up and cause-effect. As in any entrepreneurial effort, some projects work better than others. Some fail and are analysed to see if they could be better used at a later date. The long-haul strategy needs to be prepared for setbacks along the way and adapt accordingly to changing market conditions. Market conditions are defined as world geopolitics and events. Regional events; such as an immigration phenomenon, persistent wars, or leaders who last for decades. Building soft power always requires building a Soft-Power-Strategy; defining short, medium, and long-term goals, as well as operative tactics and tools to reach those goals. Tools can range from aid to media ownership, language schools to private charter jets and financial institutions. The content of influence can be anything, imagination as the limit.

Just as leadership is a mental state of mind, a sports performance is both physical and mental fervour, the spirit from Los Angeles and Seoul to London Olympics. Winning in sports equals the performance of an economy, a belief to advance further, building future for a nation. This ups the nation state brand that gains positive attention in the eyes of institutional lenders, lowering interest rates and tension in international markets.

In today's world, the United States is slightly declining in absolute soft power. But it maintains its relative positive status of smart power, and therefore influence, compared to China, the EU, and Russia. People in Europe, the masses and elites, no longer find America's past actions fully acceptable, adorable, or charming. The U.S. spends four hundred times more on hard power than on soft power. Hard power may present notification, but the attractiveness of a country is based on its culture, political ideas, policies, resources, and ideals. The United States faces a situation where its appeal lags in specific regions and countries, while its positive charm still works in many other regions, especially in specific fields in societies. Charm, as with any group of people, sports team, company, or department needs to be revitalised from time to time. If there is a brand catastrophe of some kind the brand management needs to put in the extra effort and use a humane approach in admitting their mistakes. It's a way to find reconciliation among the masses is information presentation through mass-media. China exerts soft power efficiently in long-term strategic planning. The model fits to build influence both near- and far-abroad.

Reference:

1. Hytönen Kaisa, Suomen maabrändäyksen taustasyyt ja toimintamallin kehittäminen, 2012, Lapin Yliopistopaino (in Finnish).

Nation Branding

Branding of a national state has multiple windows of presentation and each window has many dimensions. The image of a country and its identity is a complex web of analysis, which presents each operator depending on its viewer and the viewer's own international brand. Scattered information and its low bar access have changed how countries are perceived. Since the early 1990's freedom of speech has increased globally. Since the late 1990's communication and access to information, the weight of economic success, and eventual rise of the informed individual, that has abundance of information at hand, anytime and anywhere. The value of country branding has become essential. Countries have changed themselves towards a facilitator of economic guidance. Even arts and culture have changed toward value building and creation of cultural influence, such as the network of Guggenheim Museums. Branding of a country requires an economic wealth of culture, values, and knowledge. Also legacy and heritage, as well as history in general, play a strong role in brand creation.

Everyday society, administration, offices and organizations, that maintains the pillars of power in society are essential to maintain a frame elements of a country's brand, maintenance and creation. Positive and tempting country branding pulls investments, top international talent, and global corporations that want their headquarters based in a specific country. Tourism and culture bring in many visitors, who again, spread a message of positive or negative feeling for a country. This accumulates to political influence and well-being for citizens. Attention plays an essential role in country branding; by rising above the noise people see and hear about a person, corporation, and a country. This may not be about controlling the world per say, but it is about having influence in matters and guiding others in their actions. The elite leaders of a country need to have aligned interests in regards to the outcome of the brand process. What is the intention and what are the desired achievements of the branding process? There needs to be a strategy, created for success, with a differentiated and simplified message for focused distribution. The international system creates a framework for the brand process. The starting point is differentiation and desire for influence. The outcome is the implied politics that first define and then execute the branding process. Brand is about messaging and experience that the mental imagery carriers and delivers to its recipient, the nation state brand audience. The brand of a nation is mostly a mental state; there is no physical product to offer. The aim is clear, to promote the national image. In power terms, nation state branding sits in the cross section of soft power and smart power, resulting in a cultural identity.

The success rate of a nation state can be evaluated by GNP, fame, wars fought, and rankings by various statistics. Also exports, administration, cultural elements, demographics, tourism, and investments carry weight in country comparison. Lately, immigration has also played a role that reflects to security, that reflects onwards to brand of a city, region, country but also to leaders themselves. Economical tendency, political, and administrative features are part of nation state branding.

Talent is essential in building wealth and a long-term competitive advantage. Proper education for public and private school students plays a key role in creating individuals that are able to outsmart others in the global competition. Scandinavian schooling produces skilled people in vast quantities with top-tier capabilities to out innovate their peers. This is essential in the global race for success. Competing for the best talent is even more important for a country in globalization. Resources are also essential in creating a vast scale of well-being and natural resources. Corporate taxes are part of the brand package. Economic stability in general is essential to make the grade in global competition. Eventually success in the broadest meaning creates a good country brand. Success is achieved by having citizens achieve their economic dreams and prosperity. Not only economically, but also with a true feeling of pride for their citizenship.

The international political arena values problem solving instead of creation. Other competitors in the global country competition can accuse weaker countries of having inadequate means to drive their competitive efforts. As in the Olympics, optimal achievements are not only about one's optimal performance; they are also about psychological influence towards competitors. Breaking a world record is optimal performance, but winning an Olympic medal is both high performance achievement and psychological influence within the minutes before performance and the seconds or minutes during. The country branding committee sits between the desired outcome of the branding process, the elite of the nation create a simplified message that related strategy then defines, with methods and tactics for execution.

How influence is built?

Power is the ability to persuade people to get the outcomes one wants, with three different approaches: coercion (force), cash (greed), and persuasion (lure). Force is a clear form of hard power. A financial transaction is balance between greed and fear, and persuasion is where attraction and seduction meet, creating soft power. Winning hearts and minds is essential, and in the age of social networks frictionless information flow is feared by some leaders.

Soft power does not automate influence. Influence can be the outcome of hard power, threats, and actions or soft power of persuasion. Soft power equals multiple dimensions; it is persuasion, attraction, and silent approval of an action. It is about the attractive appearance of a thought, action, and guidance for the sender's benefit. Influence can be any combination of powers, with smart power being optimal in modern society.

Russia builds with both persuasion and coercion, depending on need. Ukraine is feeling the pain on multiple fronts, soft power in terms of defaming top politicians, from positive to negative and back to positive with random change of direction, constant change of facts to half-truths or extracting portions of facts and turning them against the topic, denial of clear facts or placing hashing alternate truths that mash into the allegations. And thus, to cause confusion and lack of clarity and human understanding of the desired subject. Medium power such as cyber-attacks, are about effecting crucial functions in society, such as turning off electricity or water distribution of a city. Hard power is direct military power projection. It can be enforced with full-spectrum of political, economic, diplomatic, informational set of tools, with mash-up of tactics such as militia without emblems and an unclear origin of military equipment. During Cold War, Russia's intentions was to outnumber and exceed any NATO capability. We see similar tendencies towards 2020's, but with near abroad influence geographic limitations. It is likely Russia will test out determination of the West, for example, with operations to and from Kaliningrad supported with full-spectrum power projection.

Influence can be built with long-term operations can last a decade, medium term operations of few months, or short strikes that are meant to appear and vanish overnight. The attraction of an influencer state can be conveyed via cultural cooperation, such as art exhibitions, language and culture schools, travel for the masses, and the like. Cooperation with multinational organizations and companies, such as joint ownership companies, agreements of timber, oil, coal, or uranium deliveries.

Diplomatic relations, elite cooperatives with first-class visits, open doors in the high level in the influence scale. These efforts may include comprehensive economic agreements and strategic partnerships. Overall it is about building an atmosphere for positive discussions. Dynamic progressing of cooperatives, to present an easy-to-sign solution, where a single nation state provides vast variety of products with easy and convenient delivery service for long term, becoming a gravitational pull of influence.

Soft power is about turning the opposing feeling and human

prejudice into acceptance, with baby steps, in the long run, so that one cannot see or feel the slow movement other than to realize that the new solution is not that bad and it is actually quite comfortable. Soft power is broad range of power as a sphere that applies to multiple areas, everything outside the traditional security elements. Soft power includes media in localized mode with any desired language, aid for infrastructure projects, or human crisis. Aid in some African countries has been sorted in such way that the local leaders benefit directly from the package, therefore giving positive acceptance to the approaching party.

Soft power is scaled from immaterial to material means, and low grade for the masses, the public, medium grade for professionals, and high grade for elites. Soft power works for both the private sector as well as governmental institutions, and individuals of both of those sectors. An essential piece of soft power are the business people. They act on field operations, actuating the tactical operations progress. China pushes Taiwan, Philippines, Vietnam, Indonesia and Japan to incrementally shrink their regional influence on South China Sea. Russia has used its regional influence to Baltic States, Hungary, Cyprus and far abroad influence towards Venezuela.

Soft power worked for the United States in the 1980's providing pop culture in motion pictures and pop songs that helped, in its own right, to tear down the Berlin Wall. In these times the United States has faced a situation where other alternatives have appeared on the game table. The American dream has lost its appeal, and Europe lead the neo liberal democracy example, but both of them, partly due to the financial crisis of 2008, lost their glamour in the eyes of the fallen middle class. When one needs to raise the question, what's next for the West, the opportunity is there for new actors to step in and perform their act of tempting charm, and see who's willing to go along. In mid 1990's most people ranked the United States as the leading country in the world with a highly admired culture. After the September 11, 2001 attacks the United States took a turn for worse in terms of global branding but the slump of the American brand lowered with the pictures from Abu Ghraib prison and Guantanamo prison imagery. After the 2008 financial crisis Europe and America lived on with their broken dreams, the unwanted crisis, and unemployment. This was seen as an opportunity by the terrorist groups, who glorified a false picture of a glamour and glittery war against the United States, which was a mere facade painted by thousands of recruiters in social media. Soft power worked for each party in their times, for their efforts and aims. The problem that America faced was that its soft power did not work anymore because its hard power became its soft power. After establishing a learning curve of the United States' success, Russia gradually asserted its soft power initiative, increasing it gradually since 2005. Opinions of Washington fell in Southeast Asia and Europe, and the window of opportunity rose for both China and Russia. They are both strong at their borders. In 2010's, Russia and China became self-aware of their place in the world, creating domestic pressure with nationalistic themes, and eventually leaders in these countries enticed the overall internal force for them to emerge.

The United States' sanction oriented policies, expanding its legal punitive reach globally, its commercialized criminal industry and having severe integral ethnicity, and disintegrated political field, caused the western to repel the former cooperation. The demise of the United States relative power; hard power wars that the United States keeps losing, soft power operations that fail due to hard power problems, and also alienation of its long term allies in the fight against terrorism. The world is watching a great relative power slide from the United States towards China and Russia, but also Islamic Middle-East states.

Implications of Power build-up

Thinking of charm, it can also turn against the proposing influencer, the more the sender reveals of its ambitions, the less the audience favors its message. Thinking of a presidential candidacy, the more a nominee reveals details along the campaign, the less people stand for him. Attacking other candidates isn't going to solve your problem either. The option is to change the proposal all together, fairly radically bring a truthful new you in front of the electorate. It depends on your new message and proposal to increase the chances to win, or you are toast and better save the campaign money for some other campaign on some other level, industry, or border depending on your business. The opportunity for the sender of the message is how people change their mindset about a candidacy, proposal, partnership, or a nominee. To be a game changer, i.e. something totally different than what viewers and listeners are used to.

The power in our times rises rapidly, but it is difficult to maintain - we live in times of state level influence, open personal narcissism, followers, and a too-open society that is easy to exploit by professional groups that understand the dynamics and have the resources to exploit communities. The challenge is not to achieve and gain power for a moment but to keep it in the long run. The masses get bored quickly in the era of Snapchat and other instant give-me-it-all media culture, and therefore people will be tempted by any new and attractive global theme.

China's strategy includes cooperation with countries that have an ailing partnership with America. China offers bilateral relationships to Sudan, Venezuela, Philippines, Cambodia, Uzbekistan, and Indonesia. All of these countries prefer running their societies from the top in pragmatic means, and limited openness in the economy. China provides considerable aid to the Philippines, over multiple times of the amount of U.S. Russia supports Belarus, its vassal, which is likely to become part of

Russia in the long run. China also financially supports Thailand by buying a surplus of Thailand's agriculture products, while it promotes Chinese companies and provides study trips to China for high-grade decision-makers. At the same time, China down-plays its influence for its partner's regards to concerns of its global might, with increased budgets for diplomacy with a peaceful concept. China and Russia have presented cultural cooperation with exhibiting art in Western museums and organizing museum exhibits. During these events Russia has expanded its RT television channel, which is now approaching the levels of viewers of the BBC. Chinese language schools have been available in Southeast Asian Universities and CCTV broadcasts have been expanding in the region, as well as worldwide. China is luring Southeast Asia away from Washington's influence, at the same time the United States tightens visas for students, rising the bar to approaching the West.

Eroding and Degrading Power

When finding ways to de-influence an existing or expanding power of the adversary, it is essential to pull out from an existing pile of power levels, instead of trying to operate by force. Persuasion can be used to deny one's skills, contributing thoughts, knowledge, and resources from the opponent's power exercise. Each power pillar needs to be persuaded separately with an individual tactic planned by, and for, each operator and type of power they hold. It is essential that the holder of power does not feel threatened or undervalued as a person, quite the opposite is required for successful persuasion. If the influence is successful, members of the power-pillar will self-create ways to withdraw their support of the executive branch. It is therefore essential to influence the members of the pillar, instead of operate by force. Each of the members know by themselves the best methods to operate in their field of operations. This can happen by openly disregarding advice, guidance, and rules, or by subtly disobeying orders and rules. The degrading of order execution may happen at alternate pace, and at a very slow pace the people involved, who have the power of the pillar, can hardly see the degrade of their power in their field. Humans are very efficient at seeing rapid movement, but extremely bad at noticing slow degrading or accelerating changes; such as carrying out an order incompetently. As the degrade starts to expand and gain momentum, it is usually easier to find others who are willing to join the movement, as this scenario of survival instinct, or mass behavior and mass hysteria, can be experienced in a fashion similar to a flock of birds escaping as single bird escapes.

When moving from pillar to pillar, to weaken the generalized power, it is essential to understand that coercion by force is less effective than persuasion by lure. One can see this scenario in practice when an individual and their cause is threatened, instead of persuading them by their human elements of a person, having children, family, or being humane. To succeed, it is important to define the ways power is exercised in your society, and prioritize the pillars and estimate the structural solidity of them.

From the power holder's perspective, the police are the most important source of power. As they maintain law and order, they have essential knowledge and capability to keep society stabile. The military is equally important. However, usually power itself is prioritized by the holder either towards military or police. Civil servants are part of the power pillars and they usually create a large administrative entity, the state servants, also called in, common terms, bureaucrats. In many, but not all democratic countries, this group is often seen as inefficient in the public eye. However, civil servants, and institutions, have a large skill set and vast knowledge of society and its functions and can impose cut-offs in terms of stopping most processes in the society. It is essential to understand that if government organizations withdraw their support from the executive branch most functions in society stop instantly. Other essential parts of power pillars are education related functions and organized religion, media, and the business community. In all of these sections, participating young people, students, stand together with their families. Governments depend greatly on teachers as they keep students organized and serve as role models. Younger generations adopt the values and guidelines given at home but also at educational institutions. Therefore, it is essential to realize that the education sector stands at the forefront of nonviolent movements in societies, as typically students have no children or assembled family set-up. They have time, energy, and efficient communication to perform fast projection towards power disintegration. In regards to media, students have efficient means and innovative knowhow how to disseminate their messages to their peers. Quite often media and imposed limitations are the first to be targeted to limit and deny access to electronic communication services. Business pillars' most important function is profit, and they provide supplies that the government cannot produce or import in sufficient quantities. The investment and promise of a better future are key terms to operate with the business entities.

When masses of people from various pillars transfer their motivation away from the pillar, that part of society becomes inefficient and eventually stops operating. This weakens the central government, or the infiltrated external power that tries to take over a country, or an organization such as a corporation. Rulers in general can only rule, the decisions they make are enforced by the institutions and their granted support. People in society, whether that is a corporation, nation state, or a pact, issue energy, dynamics, time, resources, skills, and knowledge to their leaders, without that consent the executives cannot rule.

Reference:
Propaganda, Persuasion and Deception, Over 1.120 selected quotations for the ideological sceptic, Laird Wilcox, 2005
Soft Power by Joseph S. Nye Jr. 2014
Is the American Century Over by Joseph S. Nye Jr. 2014
The End of Power by Moses Naim
A Guide To Effective Nonviolent Struggle.

Charm of China

China, and its participation in the global word order, has catalyzed an irreversible trend of participation in the global exchange of ideas, influence, and participation to extend Chinese reach overseas, near abroad, and far abroad. The economic rise and explosion of wealth has enabled China's capabilities that allow the country to build and defend its reach in global security affairs. This presents a new level of normal for China in its elevated security activity with a global scope. China's strategy is based on a holistic view of security, both traditional and non-traditional; terrorism, delivery of imports and exports on sea-lanes, piracy, and peacekeeping. The list of hard values and power projection is to build a strong presence along its near abroad waters such as the South China Sea expansion to islands turned into air and naval bases. The official terminology presents all this as 'contributing to world peace and support of the developed countries'. China's normal is a strategy and an implemented ambitious vision of global security participating in active role beyond traditional limits of Japan, Taiwan, Philippines and Indonesia. China's three-pillar model encompasses engage, shape and balance as the security activates of the country. China has positioned itself towards influence for all of South China Sea. It is keenly looking at Washington's response and aperture to present itself in regards to China's limited 'expeditionary status' beyond near shore towards global blue waters by 2030.

The daily battle in China is fought between the society and information what the masses are fit to search, see, read and understand. China is in a state of rapidly progressing economy and revitalized society that craves a wide variety of entertainment and information in multiple forms and levels, while the party-state holds a steady grip of indefinite political power. The state-controlled system of mass persuasion is effective in controlling information flows and controlling the masses, even though the state still lives midway between a desire of total control and globalization and information revolution.

China's leaders are bridging towards economic and strategic partnerships. China's soft power in the region of South China Sea is built with both hard and soft power. Hard power is built to ensure capabilities within an area, but at the same time China builds soft power by persuasion. Soft power makes China look less frightening, now that it is building a strong military presence and economic strength.

Chinese control of information is vast, ranging from dissemination of information to creations. This includes schooling, primary schools and middle schools, and vocational education, newspapers, radio stations, broadcast and on demand television, publishing houses and tight control of authors, and magazines with media offices of various sorts. The system also includes control over education organization, musical groups, film theaters, drama clubs and theaters, culture and art exhibitions, libraries, and exhibition halls of various types. Every information creation or conveying organization is under total control. Limiting and controlling information is half the story, and other side is about creating information by the propaganda system where it creates proactive propaganda, disseminating the kind of information the nation state believes citizens should be receiving and inserting it into various section of the demographics of the nation. The Communistic Party of China desires and aims for a harmonious society that shapes and educates the citizenry. Chinese propaganda is divided into internal and mass propaganda, where the internal version (intra-party) is aimed at party members exclusively, structured into party publications, party schools, cadre training courses, study sessions by local party committees, and national propaganda campaigns, with the main types of medias being newspapers, books, and journals. For all content there is a review system that relies on self-censorship rather than systematic browse-through of everything, which would be impossible with the volume of online media.

The mass propaganda in China is an important instrument and a tool for the Communistic party's means of control. In the age of mass information flows, no structure can filter out every piece of unwanted information that present a constant system of ecommerce, technology, and public sophistication in the use of consumer devices and services. This declines the Party's influence in China, and its citizen's understanding of events and beliefs, both domestic and foreign. First, the masses question the messages by sender, then the message itself becomes unbelievable and questioned. Any nation state has only partial control in people's thinking and in shaping their ideas and what they believe in, losing key controlling functions, then losing its legitimacy, and eventually the crucial battle over minds and hearts.

The current growth rate of China's military is half of that of the United States. China is building its second battle carrier group, but is still two decades behind the U.S. strike force. However, Chinese capabilities will greatly enhance regionally in the South China Sea and the Western Pacific in the very near term. Also, China has asymmetric capabilities in space, as is India, both reaching towards Russia's and the United States' capabilities in longer term.

For the first time since the Second World War, the United States is facing a situation where its appeal comes second, in an important region of the South China Sea. China has expanded its sphere consistently for a decade to various African countries, investing over $200 billion with over a million emigrants now working in Africa. Today over 70 percent of Thais consider China the most important trade partner, leaving the long time strategic ally of the United States behind. China has benefitted from the United States missteps in multiple wars in Iraq and Afghanistan, but also a slow reaction to the Asian financial crisis and to post 9/11 terrorism unilateral strategy. China has rehearsed its soft power, its ability to persuade by trade and cultural cooperation rather than coercion. Soft power is persuasion for elites and masses, in the demographic vertical. A wide variety of items from immaterial to material, therefore covering all aspects of a society. Culture, aid, art, language courses, cultural visits, diplomacy, investments, and business people themselves make all this happen. The participation of multinational associations and companies is performed by Chinese and local businessmen and women to propel their personal wealth by promoting activity between the nations of Thailand, the Philippines, Indonesia, Hong Kong, Macau, Vietnam, South-Korea, and Japan – all this creates a gravitational pull of both cultural and economic soft power.

For China, soft power is about all elements of a society, outside the security realm. The broad approach to interact with a nation, is to implement mass persuasion tactics that are part of a larger strategy. To lure a society for friendly terms, out from the umbrella shield of a traditional ally. All this, to enable business people, the actors on the field, to make an impact on the society in a positive sense. The South China Sea and its coasts are a natural area to extend Chinese power, as it is its near abroad area, at least the northern part of the area. At the same time, China is determined to push out the traditional power players of Japan, Taiwan, and of course the United States. Beijing's society doctrine is based on a win-win bilateral philosophy, a cooperation between any regional nation, by listening to their thoughts and problems and trying to solve them one by one. An example of this policy is by signing the Southeast Treaty of Amity and Cooperation, and committing itself for integrity and solidarity on the South China Sea. China focuses on countries that have their bilateral trade with the U.S. in decline. With Cambodia and the Philippines, but also outside the region with Venezuela, Nicaragua, Sudan, and Uzbekistan, whose ties with Washington have deteriorated, China stepped in and bolstered its relations with these countries. China also plays the soft power game in Indonesia and the Philippines, where China's aid is considerably higher than the United States.

China ties its aid and cooperation into soft values, but clearly identifiable and calculable targets, such as the promotion of Chinese companies and cultivation of politicians and decision-makers. Chinese officials are active in their visits and presence, for example to Thailand and Cambodia. China also uses soft tactics aimed for the masses, museum exhibits to promote Chinese admiral Zheng He, that never conquered any nations. Chinese language schools, university cooperation with broadened visa allotments, and CCTV, the Chinese broadcast television, are all tools to get presence and influence for nations and their politicians in the region. All this, while the United States has tightened its screws and decreased its cooperation between the countries in the region. While Beijing is building air bases in the South China Sea islands it intends to dominate the regional waterways and control the sea area in total – implement a "Monroe Doctrine" of China in the South Asian region, and having the local powers dump the United States as a strategic partner. There has been progress, with Chinese business people receiving treatment that was exclusively for the US earlier. There has also been treatment of isolation, as China has issued a policy to reward countries that are willing to isolate Taiwan, and keeping Japan from regional support in regards to trade and politics. In the worst-case scenario, China's progress is slowed but the momentum is there and growing.

While all strategic planning and cooperation, luring and charm is being built and conveyed, the day-to-day lives of those in China face a growing variety of social problems, with a rapid rise of people over 65 who end up living alone, which now accounts for a fifth of all households living by themselves, with women being a majority in this section as they outlive their husbands. Nursing homes are extremely rare in China, the typical model is to stay with a family as over 66% of elderly live. But an increasing number of people are living with only basic companions, such as a radio, even though many of the younger generations live by themselves, older generations are used to living with their partners. Family has been the main frame of how the Chinese portray themselves, as family has been an extended, calm, and safe extension living in single house or apartment. In China there is a saying; "raise your children for your later days." Over two-thirds of pensioners live with their family, a figure that is far greater than in western countries.

In the mid 2020's Chinese pensioners will account for over one fourth of the population (1). This will be a huge task for the pension system that currently has millions of people without any income. In the mid 2010's the number of working people per pensioners is 8 by 2050 the figure will decline to just 2.5. The amount of residential care is growing but is far behind the need, over 5.8 million beds for people over 60, accounting only for 3% of the need. All this reflects the rising rates of suicidal behavior, as people over 65 commit half of all suicides, as living alone as an elder in China is isolating them from the society. While at the same time Beijing is looking beyond its borders for greater investment and economic cooperation as well as trade opportunities. Until now it has had limited return on investments in its bid to build soft power in Africa and Latin America.

Reference:
China's great game: Road to a new empire, Financial Times, Oct. 12.
The Diplomat, June 5th, 2015.
State Council Information Office Issues "China's Military Strategy", Xinhua, 2015 May 26th.
The Economist, August 29th, 2015.
China's Charm: Implications of Chinese Soft Power, June 2006
Chigaco Journals, The China Journal, January 2007.
Soft Power by Joseph S. Nye Jr. 2014

Scandinavian Model

Defined as "socialist democracy" by Bernie Sanders, better phrased as social democracy. The middle ground between capitalism and socialism, is back as prevailing taste. After a lagging decade of economic growth in the West, people, especially under 30 year-old Americans, are looking at it more favorably than capitalism (1). Social democracy is more compassionate about a middle ground economy than an all-out capitalistic version. The middle ground is actually the Scandinavian model, where it is essential to understand that social democracy is not socialism, and far from communism. The Scandinavian model has its benefits, as it relies on high taxing and regulations in the private sector, but it does not endorse government acquisition of banks or corporations (even though bank bail-outs have eaten quite a lot of government funds), and individual are in charge of their wealth creation, but public sector spending is much heavier than in the Unites States. Competition is essential in creating better, more efficient goods and services, and to avoid lag and slack in the markets. The judicial system protects distortions in market economics, such as fraud, corruption, and tax evasion and protects immaterial rights that propel innovation. All this being put together for life, freedom and liberty.

For all this to work there needs to be economic freedom, which has been in decline in the United States since the 2000's and is becoming a mixed economy instead a true capitalistic El Dorado. Free trade is crucial to economic growth and isolatable measures will cripple any modern nation state, even America. Scandinavian countries have freer trade than the United States in terms of exports and imports, however the size of government spending and regulation is a fifth higher in most Scandinavian countries. Both sides of the lawn are green, the blend of government vs private sector is a matter of taste and preference. An individual can create their own luck in both types of economies. However, free high-quality education up to university level is essential as a competitive resource. To become an active participant in the future decades in an automated-everything-society, the level of skill is what counts. America may turn towards isolationism, but how about totally opening up borders between the United States and selected European Union countries, for friction free trade and movement?

References:
1. Tupi Marian, German Chelsea, Human Progress, 2016-02-17 (1)

5. Society Doctrine

From Media Doctrines to Society Doctrine

Doctrine is a solid core of a story, a manufactured threat, a psychological framework for the leadership of a nation. The intention of a doctrine, an article of faith, is to ensure wide margins when decoding state and status of events taking place near-abroad and far-abroad of a nation-state. Then to ensure operations have loose connection and limitations in regards to the use of warfare. In business terms, doctrine defines constant monitoring and evaluating the competitive landscape, and justifies counter actions in competition and forced changes in market conditions. Whereas, mass persuasion, also known as propaganda, is an appeal to emotion and is used for the purpose of swaying the opinions of the targeted audience with a defined set of methods and techniques. The overall strategy, implementing the story of threat, in which mass persuasion is provided, together with a variety of coordinated means through media channels, and premium media brands is the media doctrine that a nation state defines, controls, and executes in a systematic fashion. Media doctrine is part of a larger control of society in general, as pillars of power, influence towards crowds and the means and techniques of mass persuasion, all knit into an overall blanket of influence, intending to cover the whole nation-state and its functions with a society doctrine.

Cooperation by media persuasion; strategic influence is a combination of various methods and implemented tactics. Affairs, politics, advocacy, diplomacy, and psychological operations - combined with various ratios and tempo, depending on the implied situation, all together create strategic influence. In most countries the government wants to build a positive, unique, and solid image of itself, as do corporations, sports teams, and celebrity individuals alike. Opponents to the official view are depicted as populists, racist, hooligans, rebels, or the like. Larger countries such as the United States, China and Russia want to control what and how things are said about them. As we live in the times of global terrorism, a double standard of the message is intentionally implied to distanced facts away from terrorism, depending on event and claim. Terrorism can be conceived as a communication phenomenon (Mass Media and Warfare, Greg Simons) that can be classified broadly within the term propaganda. This can be split into two sections, propaganda of the deed and propaganda of the ideology. Ideology again can be defined as a doctrinal organization and management of citizenry. Also, the means to produce a political establishment and maintain the power of that organization can be included in the ideology of power.

There are various ways to interfere with news on how people feel about things and events. How citizens find news in either positive or negative light - to win the hearts and minds, or to depict a specific group of people in such ways that it serves the establishment that it is influencing. These operations can be scaled down to groups of people classified by ethnicity, location, tribal background, or gender. The ways to influence the targeted group can be many; the limitations likely can be limited by one's imagination. To influence in large scale, one needs to have the attention of the masses. One needs to cause a public spectacle in order to attract mass media attention. Terrorists cut off people's heads in medieval style, whereas as an American businessman and presidential hopeful Donald Trump says the unsaid about politicians and celebrities. These examples are intentionally created spectacles to gain attention. State actors can create propaganda by the deed, in order to create a public spectacle for attention, and then create a dialogue for the public sphere. In propaganda of the ideology, state actors influence a targeted public group that can be categorized in multiple ways, for example by citizenry or location, and then add pressure to that group with political and social ideas, which may first sound irrational, but depending on the pace, intensity, and ways of persuasion, the adversary of the past is made to look charming. After this level is achieved, the content is multiplied to other sectors of society, to influence the public with the message, that is favorable for sender's agenda.

Eventually, the final phase is to persuade the selected focus group to think and behave in a way that allows the adversary to realize its objectives. Such objectives can be, for example, to influence the public to such a state, that they vote leaders into administration that are favorable to the adversarial promotion of power. Eventual aim to control the country by bribing the elite who have been favorable to the adversary. Again, there are numerous ways to perform the overall scenario, and the targets for each level of influence, with a customized storyline and tactics to gain control of a specific group of people. Creativity and systematic operations follow a pre-written manuscript, a storyline, which has iterations of opponents' actions, with a matching counteraction, as a toolbox to fit every scenario. Hybrid tactics of power can be applied to increase and decrease the feeling of a threat towards the public creating a very efficient doctrine itself to reach the desired objectives.

Reference:
Venäjän Informaatio-psykologinen sodankäyntitapa (in Finnish) - Heidi Berger, 2010.
http://www.globalissues.org/article/352/mainstream-media-and-propaganda
China's Propaganda System: Institutions, Processes and Efficacy by David Shambaugh, The China Journal No. 57, Jan. 2007. Pp. 25-58 by Chicago Journals
Infosota by Jantunen Saara (in Finnish), 2015

Pillars, Sources and Levels of Power

What is power in society?

Power is the means to have one's way with sticks, carrots, or influence. Power can be implemented by leaders who own the society, who control the means and distribution of information. The creation and fabrication of truth divided and distributed for each class and sector in society. A blended message, that is suitable digestible to most. Power, therefore, is not an instant tool that one can use, but a combination of tools, means, content, relations, and resources, such as finance, to have the operative capability to disseminate a set of tailored messages to gain a focus group's attention, acceptance, and approval for action. Power is also required to reach the vision after the win. Freedom and justice are not to be taken for granted. If one wants power - there is a struggle and a cost to grab it. Political power is the totality of means, influences, and pressures - authority, rewards, and sanctions - to achieve the objectives of the power holder; those of the government, state, and related organizations.

In the monolithic model, the authoritarian created system wants no change in power in society. Even though power may seem monolithic, it is always multidimensional and diametrically in constant change. Individuals and society are changed, with a term of years and decades. However, when the change starts to happen in a society, it can be swift as the built pressure of change causes the uncontrolled outcome. People and power reside in the same location, therefore, they are interdependent.

In the pluralistic model, the power of the society comes from the people. Each individual is small, but the group is large in power and influence. The momentum is built around the power and volume of participants and the level of activity. When one multiplies these two the power change becomes strong and if the counterforce is weaker, the result changes. Rulers only have the power that people, in masses, provide them. Change may come in slight increments, but with pressure, it will eventually cause structural changes. In organizations, there may be a need for face-saving procedures by reseating leaders. Power may seem strong and invincible, but it is often fragile, dispersed, and in the hands of a few in an organization. A change can happen, without violence or force, in a coordinated way through strategic planning.

Reference:
Adaptation from The Politics of Nonviolent Action - Gene Sharp.
The Economist.

Sources of Power

1. **Legitimacy and Authority**
   The position to give orders, present legitimacy of orders. Capability to change legitimacies.
2. **Human resources**
   Groups and organizations that follow order of the board, government, superiors or other executive power holders. The people distributing policies over society.
3. **Skills and knowledge**
   Supplied by knowledge holders, intellectuals, upper class, experts, and citizens with skill. The governing executive needs a constant flow of skills and knowledge.
4. **Material and economic resources**
   Access and control of financial, economic, communication, transportation, energy and raw materials. The groups that are dependent will less likely revolt against the governing body.
5. **Habits and values**
   Attitudes, values, traditions, culture as well as psychological, religious, ideological factors and forces that may enhance or prevent from people to act according to executive branch and rulers.
6. **Enforcement**
   The capacity of execution of breach of orders and laws. Exercise laws and execute laws and judicial decisions. Maintaining control through law approved by the people, or adjusted legal framework to operate with flexible capability of operations. Some regimes may force oppression through enforcement.

Pillars of Support

People create and run a society, nothing in it happens by itself. If people do not operate accordingly and provide the services needed for the executive branch to rule, leadership becomes impossible. If multiple supportive organizations stop providing support for the executive branch, the government is unable to control and maintain power. This comes down to day-to-day operations in the society. Infrastructure; such as traffic lights, energy. Provide heat and water for citizens, collect taxes and keep up with payments, just to name a few. The essentials for power support are the police, military, institutions, judiciary, and electoral commission. Other essential offices as education, religious institutions, media, and the business community.

What is the vision?

What becomes of the society after the win, on the opposite side of power change? After the Soviet Afghanistan invasion, United States planned, prepared and executed material resources and aid for local groups to overtake Soviet forces, that had the insurmountable military force and over 100.000 men in arms boots of the ground. After providing Stinger missiles for Afghanistan troops, they started slow but steady to overcome the air superiority that Russian air force projected on them with fighter aircraft. Eventually, Russian were forced to pull out after suffering has casualties and wide financial losses by downing a fighter plane worth tens of millions with a shoulder aimed and fired rocket worth tens of thousands dollar. The economy in large scale beat the adversary, but the United States left it at that without a vision of tomorrow for the country. This caused in wide scale, women and children to be left without education, building the groundwork for terrorism in the 2010's. A schooling system, education, is essential, to have knowledge in a society and from that inability to perform propaganda that purports a false notion of matters, right and wrong.

It is essential for both genres, men and women to be able to read, think and judge for themselves, alternatively the capability to feed half-truths and lies to masses will prevail. The vision of tomorrow is, therefore, the most important piece of power change, without vision, there is no sense to push for a major change in society.

Levels of Power

Thin Power

Preparing Soft-power operations. Having individuals checked for possible operations. Combing the potential influence or adversary territory for possible resources. Theoretical discussions and gathering responses from people of influence both home and abroad (1). Recruitment from competitors and adversaries.

Soft Power

Systematic long, medium, and short-term influence creation in a geopolitical region, individual nation state, or multiple states. Near abroad or far abroad influence with popular culture, motion picture, music, brands, fashion, media of all sorts, trolls to moderate local opinion and test the response of larger audiences, sports team, and fancy venues - all this with with business people being the hands on legal operatives. Pushing the boundary of legal and unethical operations as far as possible (3). Testing the response of press and politicians, finding limits. Gaining a strong foothold to proceed swiftly and rapidly to medium and hard power as needed (2).

Medium Power

Cyberwarfare. Stealing research and development material. Systematic planning and infiltration of adversary. Open intelligence information gathering throughout the society and nation state. Profiling people, both civil and military. Systematic stealing of maps, plans, documents of decision-makers, politicians, and administrative organizations in both the government and private sectors.

Hard Power

Silent war - war with denial of being in a conflict. Delivering arms. Disregarding international contracts. Smuggling of narcotics or arms. Abusing diplomatic agreements for false operations. Intentional shakedown of a financial and stock exchange system.

Executing cyberwarfare operations - closing down electricity systems, polluting water and living resources. Creating instability among citizens. Political threats of a nuclear strike (1).

Extra Hard Power

Coup de état. Genocide. Nuclear weapons, large installations of fighter planes, bombers, attack submarines. Declaration of war. Silent war escalation with a pre-emptive global strike. Spreading diseases and biological gases. Using EMP (electronic magnetic pulse) and space weapons. Creating chaos in the target area with massive civilian casualties.

Reference:
1. Sternberg, J Robert, The Nature of Hate,
2. Naim, Moses, The End of Power,
3. Loosely based on A Guide To Effective Nonviolent Struggle.

Development of Power, 1850 - 2020

Volume business - earlier times, 1850 - 1930s

Essentials of size and scale - strongly centralized and hierarchical organization - red army. These were engines of Catholic Church. To get maximum power out of an organisation is to get a huge in size. That thinking today still plays a part in Russia's military thinking. Strong by size, and if not according to peer in every front with the West, the aim is to get enough quality and volume for victory, blended with asymmetric warfare; using local thugs, criminals, and gangs of all sorts, still patriotic in their mindset, combined with first tier modern weapons systems that have educated personnel to operate them, giving minimal assistance and training to separatists. As in business, bigger is better. Armies, churches, political parties, and universities all have benefited from sheer size. Some are even the size of a small state, such as the National Railroad Company of India, or the security services of Most Corporation in Russia in the '90s. They have used the volume of their operations and capacity to master their opponents and advance their interests.

Capital business - various capitalisms, 1940s - 1970s

The demand for large-scale, industrial, multi-unit systems began in the late 19th century. Many of the large companies were the result of the endless consolidation of smaller companies. Numerous car manufacturers merged and acquired their rivals. Also, most of the consumer names such as Coca-Cola and Pepsi are from that era, 1860-1910, as are Bayerische Motor Werke (BMW), Thyssen Group, Badische Anilin- und Soda-Fabrik (BASF), Alexandre Darracq and Nicola Romeo (Alfa Romeo), and Fabbrica Italiana Automobili Torino (FIAT Chrysler).

The dominance of these large industrial companies was later modelled by three different models of capitalism; personal capitalism derived from the United Kingdom's class culture, managerial competitive capitalism having its roots in the United States, and cooperative capitalism popular in Germany. The latter was named after cooperation with the unions. Family founded companies in the United Kingdom had more of a static role in their development, the managers in the United States took more active roles and boldly moved their corporations to benefit from mergers and acquisitions, expansion in an agile way, which wasn't common in personal driver capitalism. The independent managers had great ambition, this led to many global expansions and generation of wealth in the 20th century and it still goes on today. Separation of ownership and managers allowed the American companies to adapt more fluent ways to benefit from recruitment and flexible organisations. Talent, capital, and innovation led to combined areas such as Silicon Valley. The German model included in-depth governance in corporate management, extending from managers to the boards to shareholders. Regardless of the fact that all of these models were based on size. They were formed by capital, innovation, and the perseverance of the founder. The power derived from being small at one time, they were all small once, learning to work their ways to the top, and then managing their societies with a visible hand. In Russia distribution of power was seen as an adversary, a threat to the state itself. Communism can be perceived a system of kleptocracy due to its high rate of corruption. In Communism, all the state's resources are in the hands of couple hundred people, as it was in the Soviet Union. Russia today is run by a small group, who ensure that they receive most of the wealth in the state and benefit the most from the resources that a country has. Corruption results in inefficiencies of slack in the market economy.

Timing in business and life - modern times, 1980s

The essence of a brick and mortar business has been location. In the network economy, it is timing. If you are doing the right thing at the right time, globally, you have success. The scope of optimal opportunity changes constantly, caused by hundreds of variables, starting with the fact that societies do not function perfectly. Starting from sun's radiation, changes in atmosphere affecting weather patterns, deicing of polar caps causing the rise of water levels, food production, lack of sustainability, manufacturing of consumer goods etc. To understand what goes where education plays an important part in all this. Because the more and better you understand the world throughout, how things work, the higher chance of success an individual has. Regardless of your point of view and desire, the more you understand how the world works, the higher likelihood you have to live a higher quality of life. If you inherited a billion dollars, one can enjoy life much more by being smart and taking a lead on things. After all, the people born now will live here for only about a hundred years. It is short window compared to the billions of years this planet has evolved.

Connections and innovation, 1990s and 2010s

It matters who you know, up to a point. Would it help if one knew a leader of a country personally? Sure it would, but only up to a point. Eventually, one has to prove competence by delivering knowledge in an actionable way. What percentage of consumers understand or care if Pepsi and Burger King are owned by the same consortium? Consumers rarely care about things they do not see. It is all about the instant benefit.

Competitive landscape leaves room for the talented and innovative to benefit and find optimal solutions. Anyone talented, without any connections whatsoever, can succeed; performance is a matter of wit, dedication, and perseverance. It goes without saying that one can make life much easier by pulling strings. In the times of proliferated computing power and global distribution of mobile applications, the global market is up to the individual to capture an audience and build a business.

John D. Rockefeller, the Astors, and Carnegies understood that connections are one thing, but innovation is of the utmost importance. They teamed up with American universities to systemically promote innovation and inventiveness in America. During the second decade of the 20th century, there were nearly 30 foundations where specialists were promoting and experimenting in the research of a variety of problems, ranging from medical to socio-economical to technological challenges. In twenty years onwards the figure was in the several hundred and the foundations of American innovation was born. This was based on philanthropy at its best The crowd funding of its time gathered money by donations for inventive products and services.

Talent and how to keep it – Beyond 2020's

What matters most when building a business is not who you know, or the time you build something, or if you have the capital to build it. What matters most is who you are building something with. Unsocial behavior can be a sign of human intelligence in the conformist world. The world where one cannot be clever and perform does not provide a good fit in an organisation. When does a leader know if a new recruit doesn't fit into the organisation? Too often managers, as in this fabricated example, get to stay for too long, ousting the best talent and leaving the organisation less competitive. A good boss defines goals, is responsible, and is fair. A bottleneck remover sees what people are good at, notices challenges, and gets a team to solve them. Optimising the components to work in an efficient and friction free order is one of a good boss's main characteristics. A bad boss thinks the organisation works for him. He has no humility. He recruits and promotes only people like him, therefore causing, even more, pain in the organisation, and a lack of talent. A bad boss often times uses divide and conquer tactics. All this causes good talent to walk away, the organization functions inefficiently, there is no reach for a common goal, and people don't work as a team. In our times, the highly educated, tech-driven, social media found talent are mostly self-guiding in terms of their knowledge and performance. These people do not need micromanagement for their performance. Professionals need to have challenging tasks to make them feel worthwhile. Quick brains need challenges with individual or teamwork depending on one's preference. Introversion is not a negative trait. We do not all need to be smiling extroverts. Tasks need to fit the mindset and organisation Everyone is a human and needs to be rewarded properly. Transparency of the organisation, clarity and transparency build trust.

Reference:

1. Naim Moses, The End of Power, 2013

6. Media and Tactics

After 2004 Republican lawmakers claimed that the White House was completely disconnected from reality. The plan to pull-out from Iraq was sarcastically called an exit plan. When 2005 drew to close expenses went through the roof and casualties rose. People became skeptical of the May 2003 triumphant speech where President Bush defined "major battles to have ended."

The Bush tactics in Iraq had failed. The media imagery from Iraq had eaten up support and justification that the American public had pledged for Bush in the aftermath of the 2001 terrorist strikes. In part, the decay of influence in regards to the imagery of the "falling man" and "airplanes hitting towers" had decayed from their peak traumatic value (3), but at the same time a counter wave from the Abu Ghraib type of imagery had disoriented the public's opinion of their servicemen's integrity. The long fought war without finding perpetrator Osama bin-Laden, had declined support for the overall war-operation itself. All this changed for the positive on May 2nd, 2011, when Bin-Laden was kill-captured from an ISI, Pakistani Intelligence Service, at a safe house in Abbottabad, Pakistan.

Rhetoric of a preemptive nuclear strike sound complex. The message had a negative sentiment for the overall Iraq operation that ailed in strategy. It was simple and easy-to-digest for viewers. From an operational perspective a doctrine can be considered "a dead letter". It is the overall interpretation of asymmetric warfare, especially information operations, which define how the masses define whether progress is made for good or if the operation is waning in the minds of ordinary people. The centrality of a preemptive strike can be questioned as a whole in the United States' strategy as the scope of preemption can be exaggerated in foreign policy. Preemptive warfare is higher in priority of a security agenda than the public notices. The nuclear doctrine from

2005 defines approval of nuclear strikes against adversaries "intending" to use "weapons of mass destruction." This results in nuclear preemption, with both battlefield destruction of targets as well as providing deterrence through threat of retaliation. These stories of threat, with an inbuilt impetus, have become key points in the United States doctrine of core missions. A "global strike" capability to neutralize threats, such as Iran or North Korea, are combined cyberwarfare and information warfare, both before and after operation. The pinpointed earth penetrating nuclear bombs destroy targets deep underground. This improves preventative means of warfare success. The modern model of combine operations are; recognized threat, developed plan of action, and execute mission with ability to strike at any moment's notice in the dark corners of the world. All this by rapidly modeling character of adversary, without the need to resort to a large numbers of general purpose forces. Objectors define preventive strike model as provocative. Whereas proponents see space systems as the solution of such objections. The Reaganistic dream of a SDI - Space Defense Initiative is very operational in our era.

The OSI (Office of Strategic Influence), in cooperation with CNN (Cable News Network) broadcast television, and related on-demand television networks, help create propaganda events that benefit Pentagon's media and influence programs. The structures and names change regularly, sometimes due to public demands. Revelations, accusations and bad mouthing, support field operations. Information operations of various kinds, anything from generics such as "the sky is going to fall," to complex ongoing scheduled schemes, supported with inhumane messages such as "the Iraqi soldiers stole the incubators from babies and left them on the hospital floor to die," guide recipients minds. Broad acceptance of ground operations increases success of guerrilla warfare. Propaganda messages such as *Nayirah Testimony* have been used to gain one-sided support and defame the ethics of opponents. The previous hoax message of babies has been created by American Hill & Knowlton for the Kuwaiti government in 1990 (2). In fact, many patients, including babies, died as hospital staff left premises and fled, but Iraqi forces did not steal the equipment as was claimed.

Information warfare requires a systemic attempt to control public discourse (3). There is a need for careful strategic and operational plans of deception, with clarity of tactics to be used to counter influence operations and strategic deception as tools of influence. The Bush doctrine defines goals for information warfare, which are based on media tactics such as denial, degradation (defame), deceit, disruption, destruction, and exploitation of these tactics. Depending on the interpretation of this set of tactics, it is sometimes included with a distortion of media messages, defaming adversarial individuals. The essential piece of tactical maneuvers include obfuscation. By obfuscating the status of the situation by adding various sets of events, brings news elements to the viewer to weight. To perceive, interpret, reason, valuate, memorize, and learn for further comparison of facts, are essential pieces to recognize propagandistic messages. Recipient should compare content on a timeline. When events are created and messages are altered. How the discourse changed in a constant mix of perspectives? The change of tempo and the information of the message are key elements in notifying citizens of propagandistic operations for influence. One can enforce these tactics with the existence of wishful thinking and psychological denial. Mash up pessimism or optimism, bind it with disinformation, intently to enforce or lessen adversarial thoughts. When multiples of such thoughts are seeded into adversarial minds, the sender can influence opponent by swinging in the mindset. Then gently advance towards higher confidence, for example, in events regards to European refugee crisis management between Germany and Russia. The humane thinking of German leadership was exploited by the Kremlin with influence tactics. This eventually revealed true intentions of Russia bombing refugees to seek cover, then producing media content of these actions, while controlling the geographical flow by productizing the measure into a set of influence tools. In Soviet deception, which the Russian model derives from, these tactics were also concealment techniques of military capabilities, the *maskirovka*, (1) including the doctoring of production and consumption statistics to deceive NATO of their economic capabilities and the military spending of the gross national product, items that were estimated far higher than they actually were upon the Soviet implosion of 1990. The principal goal of any regime, Russia included, is to convince the opponent that their intentions alter from reality. In terroristic messages in the Middle East, Nicaragua, Cuba, and Venezuela the CIA is a synonym for imperialism, which can be blamed for anything, as the evil that represents the corrupted West.

Reference:
1. Lenczowski, John, Themes of Soviet Strategic Deception and Disinformation, 1987
2. https://en.wikipedia.org/wiki/Nayirah_(testimony)
3. University of Turku – American Study Group lectures Jan-Mar, 2015.

Tendencies of Thought

Influence in media through deceptive measures can be successful, at least to start with, because of our tendencies to deceive ourselves. The most successful strategic deceptive campaigns seek for existing tendencies. Then, the intention is to strengthen and exploit the prebuilt engagement of mirror-image perception. In mirror-image perception recipients attribute the adversary behavior as we would attribute it to ourselves i.e. "be in the adversary's shoes." However, that may sometimes prove extremely difficult as the opponent may deceive us into thinking that they present themselves as their true selves, instead, what may come as a surprise is that the adversary has been feeding disinformation all along, and therefore the perception that we had in the beginning is proven totally wrong.

As an example, Soviet deception intended to display Soviet leadership as a western system. Projection outside the country; concepts of peace and war, fair play in general, and common human decency, where all viewed as western values, causing an automated deceit of tendency, creating automated values of illusionary motives and desires.

Strategic thinking and deceptive thoughts tend to take the advantage of wishful thinking and psychological denial. People living in a Western lifestyle tend to evade the truth of ugly realities. Optimism and pessimism in our minds tend to be guided towards outcomes much worse than they actually are. Opposite thoughts of desire, towards overly optimism. Staying neutral and realistic is typically difficult for humans, as we are built to like and dislike matters, especially in the narratives regards to mass information.

Mass Persuasion - Methods and Techniques

Tactical operative media tools

A nation state media doctrine can be defined by five major definitions; denial, distort, deceit, defame and diversion. These rules of information guidance intend to benefit by exploiting changes of information pace and angle of perception of recipient. The intention is to break out from general media noise and leave a trail of a story that inflicts human perception. Disinformation is typically difficult to probe and define, as news and facts are manipulated with an altered tone and perspective. The intent is to create sufficient change of information tempo. People are recipients of information flow that increases at a constant rate. Recipients do not recognize influence events in large volume. This gives the aggressor the opportunity to further push their efforts to create a sphere of influence, with a wide toolset of means. Sender can offense messages, such as the airline shoot down in multiple ways. Denial of participating in the attack, denial of clear visual facts, regardless of facts from the perpetrators themselves. Even though perpetrator sends social media messages to Twitter that confirms accused actions, they may still any event that does not benefit their agenda. Such media doctrine gives nearly unlimited tools to mix the ways media can be manipulated. Anything from changing the direction of the story's flow and narrative, from cooperation to denial, then back to cooperation but with modified content. A story can be offered in a variety of scenarios so that the public cannot select any specific right one from the offered selection. The sender of mass propaganda infiltrates the global media, partly with global distribution of its messages and partly with alternative events that confirm earlier actions. Falsified messages with alternative truths of who, what, where and why, are then injected into media flow. The intention is to confuse the viewer away from the actual series of events. The large scale deception of the events may disgrace victims by denial of investigations to access a geographical area or a building.

Methods

Mass persuasion, is appeal to emotion used for the purpose of swaying the opinions of targeted audience with a defined set of methods and techniques.

Unison hysteria - Encouraging people to think or act in some way because other people are doing so; all people are hysteric, about a growing threat of the adversary on television, it is patriotic to sing along and support leaders in fight for our country.

Luxury appeal - Making claims, one should act or think in a socially approved way according to high social status achieved with with related action, such as: sports car - feel of luxury, dynamics for those who afford the upscale lifestyle.

Vagueness - Promoting or challenging opinions by using words that are so vague, or so poorly defined as to be almost meaningless; try our new all-improved product.

Strong wordings - Using words with strong language connotations, or associations, is the use of words charged with emotion. Transfer - Making an illogical association between one thing and something else that is generally viewed as positive or negative.

Credibility - Having an unqualified person endorse an opinion, for example, in a news television broadcast (so called experts), product, action or opinion.

Diversion - It is advisable to avoid mass persuasion in one's own speeches and writings. But to recognize, alert and counteracts when noting persuasive messages being used in connection with real life events, such as elections and catastrophes. Notice these techniques when watching broadcast or on-demand television, reading news sites, blogs, or reading prints like magazines or newspapers.

Reference:
    Wilcox, Laird, Propaganda, Persuasion and Deception, Over 1.120 selected quotations for the ideological sceptic, 2005

Comparison - Russian and United States influence tactics

Essentials of information warfare are; intelligence, influence and overview of theatre-war status - influence being the most crucial combat tools. It is essential to see and understand the big picture, instead details (1). There are deep differences between Russian and American information warfare, especially when comparing consequences of media presence. "Obnoxious West" is an underdog in media presence, there is never enough confessions made, especially when the adversary keeps on fueling media messaging with cause of eternal blame (2).

Russian ways
- Based on Soviet Deception tactics (1).
- Use of media tactics without boundaries.
- Constant battle, relentless waves of influence.
- Scheduled operations, systematic approach.
- Getting caught has no effect, everything can be denied.
- Multiple truths, based on discourse.
- Actions, messages, acts have no need to concede.

United States ways
- Actions have immediate humane, forbearing ethical consequences.
- Causes instant reaction in audience, the citizens.
- Lack of image, causes rising crisis.
- Explanations, requests and demands from administration, authorities and associations.
- Self-mortification, atonement, apologies (2).
- Declarations for absolute truth with humane processing.
- Demands and declarations of moral hazard.

Reference:

1. Lenczowski John, Themes of Soviet Strategic Perception and Disinfomration, 1987 and 2006.
2. Jantunen Saara, Infosota, 2015.

Messaging Methods

Defaming of respected individuals in society is typically a prominent national leader, respected politician, investor, corporate chairman or a union leader. By defaming such a figure in a society, the adversary gains ground be degrading opinions and leadership that the individual presents. Defaming can be done by inventing and planning crimes that are bogus, fabricating extra marital affairs or proving the person wrong even with irrelevant facts that never were or took place. The sender of propaganda can make up events, scenery and place images that have no connection to claimed events, have no related people in them or simply have nothing to do with the blame generated and distributed by the controlled media channels. Repression is another negative tool, to hold back facts of factual events. The sender of propaganda can hold back from constant flow of specific information. That can be used as a tool to be used when the time is right, as to store the story for time most beneficial for the sender. Time decay is function where the benefit is created from passing of time as media information burdens recipients mind with information fatigue in the eye of the beholder. News item to degrades over time as it is treated aged leaning towards being irrelevant. Information ages eventually to zero value. In some cases, such as the 9/11 event, information is considered vital for society as it is therefore emphasized and refreshed over time. In obfuscation, the messages are mixed from truths, to half-truths and onwards to fabricated nonsense. Presenting these messages in non-sequenced way, so that the composition has a function to obfuscate the desired message, but the content set in random order manually so that no system can reverse engineer the sequence to a formula, because there is no formula. Eventually there is confusion. Systematic intention to confuse the viewer, with blame and related facts, the sender of propaganda can create a set of mixed messages. This fabricates a problem, but self-creates a solution served as needed. Problems blended with constant change, with a predefined and clear solution as a savior for situation.

Reference:
Kurlantzick, Joshua, Loosely based on Carnegie Endowment Policy Briefs
Naim, Moses, The End of Power
Jantunen Saara, Infosota (in Finnish), 2015
Adapted from, Discussion of Richards J. Heur, Jr., personal communication with Gordon Mitchell, 9 July 2005.

How to notice deceptive influence messages?

During a campaign of influence of news broadcast, when messaging tempo is swift, but changing, there may be intent of obfuscation, to confuse the recipient. When the content of the message changes according to media manipulation tactics, viewer can recognize the overall attempt to influence the recipient, by following the line of change in the message based on events and tempo of presentation, then comparing message and how its changes based on facts presented on other news channels. Unnatural change in the message content reveals the influence attempt. Quite often recipient of influential messages may notice the same story being evaluated from multiple angles, estimated and evaluated by several specialists, regardless of their true capacity to give statements (1). Information warfare has no boundaries to present true intent or absolute truth, this gives sender of influence an edge, compared to sincere broadcast of information. The message content itself, claims and "news items" can spread from simple truths to total lies, or mixes in between, typically appearing in nonsystematic fashion, to keep realism in the sequence of events.

Reference:

1. Jantunen Saara, Infosota, 2015.

Simplified Example Flow

Activity - any major event, natural disaster, accident, capture, refugee crisis, etc. (1)

1. Sender: Event message = **influence effort**
2. Recipient: Denial with counter message, explanation = **denial**
3. Recipient: Counter message with new interpretation distanced from fact = **distortion**
4. Recipient: Counter message with added defaming information of sender = **defame**
5. Sender: New perspective, distanced from original event message and added new outrageous claims = **obfuscation effort, plus re-influence**.

The intent is to confuse the enemy by psychological operations, by blurring the lines of factual information and news, public information and propaganda. It is worthwhile noting that while the official target of tactical operations can be adversarial foreign enemies, oftentimes the victims are politicians and the electorate as a whole.

Exaggeration of real events maximize event flow to create a logjam of information. This minimizes influence by denial often involving volatility and explosive reactions from media, easily losing the control of events and outcome causing an opposite result of that desired. Sometimes doctrines can backfire on the instigator, creating opposite result. By using pretexts of aggression, prerogatives of the adversary's elite class, the sender of influence messages takes great risks. Influence attempts towards societies that are run by elites are weaker and easier to build influence on, than democratic lead nations with functioning freedom of speech.

Operations of influence face constant caveats of discourse failure. Lingual bottlenecks in writing, and multitude flavors in human perception of vocabulary, easily slide towards comprehension in one's mind. Words of likelihood can guide reader towards the probability of events. The challenge lies in averting discourse failures and aversion. When war and peace hang on the message of cognitive apprehension, it is essential to select words wisely. Social media tools, both advance discussion between "us and them", while escalation of discourse risks the tide of uncontrolled path. Exponential messaging can go both ways, victoriously correct or take a turn for worse by simple mismatch of perception. The sender should have supportive messages - dialogue strategies - to clarify and carry further one's message when unexpected problems occur in debating one's perception of message, controlling the drumbeat of a conflict.

Reference:
1. Globalissues.org
   http://www.globalissues.org
http://www.overalltech.net/pub/Quotations-Propaganda.pdf

Disruptors and Exploitative Means

Media Tactics

This chapter includes a simplified list with a breakdown of methods and tactics. Disruptive methods vary and can include dozens of tactics depending on the scope and aim of an influence campaign. Idea of tactics blurs boundaries between factual information and news. Such tactics have been used by Pentagon's Office for Strategic Influence where the mission is to create disinformation and propaganda, for the use of "special plans" euphemism for mass persuasion. Some military operators have tweaked disruptors into destruction, degradation, denial, disruption, deceit and exploitation, while some call it of defame, distortion, destruction, denial, diversion and execution of the related plan. Regardless of the D's, the matter is about a disciplined tactics to modify a message that would normally be presented as it is, but now causes the viewer and listener to re-evaluate the message for sender's benefit, in systematic fashion. Pentagon's joint chiefs have issued "Joint Policy for Military Deception" it specifically orders the air Force to develop better doctrines and techniques for incorporation of obfuscation and disinformation into war plans.

Exploitation of disintegration systematically benefits from weaknesses created on the media space by above tactics. Overall exploitation mends with the operations that the tactics full fill in operations. Intent to reach strategic affluence, influence of target demographics, reaching critical level of approval among masses and eventually reaching the overall vision of the society doctrine.

Destruction of Reasoning

By mixture of methods, cause a common man to loose understanding the fact, origin of event, sequence of happenings or a combination of these. To cause havoc, one uses obfuscation and confusion in the media space. The sender of destructive messages has the intent to create a "frustration environment" where viewer loses track of what's happening and jumps to next news item.

Denial of Truth

Shooting of a Boeing 747 jumbo jet passenger plane (KAL 007) over Sakhalin cape from a Russian SU-15 fighter plane, was multiyear discussion in 1982 and a partial cause for the Reagan administration to react by spending that the adversary could not keep up with. Slightly over thirty years later, shooting down a comparable sized Boeing 777 (MH 17) over Ukraine-Russian border area, by Russian operated; Russian made; BUK Surface-to-Air Missile broke the news for some months, then faded to other battlefront news, and financial turmoil of, should Greece stay in Eurozone or not. Nearly 300 died in 1982, causing President Reagan to call Russia part of axis of evil. Equally 300 died in 2014; causing Germany Chancellor Merkel to vaguely 'condemn' the act. This was a psychological replay of 1980's, but adapted for 2010s, as the West needed strong leaders it did not have. There was confusion and misinterpretation of adversaries acts and fogged messages. The new way to play, asymmetric warfare, constant flux of information and moving the truth from one side the other sliding the situation into information chaos where masses loose track and eventually lose interest in the smartphone screens and switch to something more entertaining.

Deceit - Falsified Content Narrative

Quick turn in course regards how the media presents and perceives other real maneuvers in the backgrounds as the attention is turned into former actions in the 1990s Balkan war and early 2000's second Gulf War. The maneuvers in the background are for example security services that operate in Ukraine while the media pushes out message of past NATO and US operations.

Denial of Messages

Denial is typically presented in world politics, regardless of events, nation states, or state unions, create claims based on their strategic needs. A direct denial works for 1/5 of the recipients, but the remainder require quite a lot of effort, sliding to the last end of 1/5 that are nearly impossible convince. Troll factories of Russia provide bloggers and messaging boards information that is supportive to state actions. These are often alternative hypothesis and actually pure lies pulling a rabbit-out-of-a-hat scenario.

Distortion - Modification of Narrative

Change of facts by lies, half-truths or presenting news with strong moderation. Then using fill-in's with full truth, total false in between the half-truth's to have the message sound like truth like. Alteration of the elements is done in sequence, consistently or randomly. Distortion modifies the original narrative creating the message closer towards the support for sender's benefit.

Diversion of Events

Diversion is based on sudden change of opinion, direction, bearing of a story. Used typically to confuse the viewer from understanding the relevance of matters and importance and rating of facts. Item connection may be loosened or tightened depending on the intention of the diversion. Operating in an environment where these factors and their planning is present can be exciting in the beginning, but become exhausting in the long term. Methods can be defined as a settled kind of procedure, usually according to a definite, established, logical, or systematic plan: the open-hearth method of making steel, one method of solving a problem. Technique is the manner and ability with which an artist, writer, dancer, athlete, lawyer, or the like employs the technical skills of a particular art or field of endeavor so as to effect a desired result. There is even an official profession to manage the adversarial message flow with counter claims and blames. The "Adversary

Perception Manager" is a position to study how foreign entities attempt to mislead regional and nationwide policymakers on critical national security issues such as participating in economic, security or a military pact. The perception can operate by previously listed methods and tactics to contact leaders of media, such a radio stations, bloggers, website management to infiltrate the media by presenting a desired message as a commercial. It is advised to avoid using mass persuasion in your own speeches and writings, but to recognize, alert, and counteract when noting persuasive messages being used in connection with real life events, such as elections or catastrophes. Notice these techniques when watching broadcast or on-demand television, reading news sites, blogs or reading a published prints like magazines or newspapers.

Defaming individuals or groups

Defaming can be used to downgrade the credibility of a group or an individual that projects opposing opinions in systematic matter against government objectives and targets, the government policy and doctrine itself. Defaming and shaming politicians and decision-makers for lessened power and credibility among nationals, voters, funders, shareholders of specific countries of groups. Defaming can be done in organizations, for example when competing for a specific spot in an organization. Defaming can be targeted towards individuals, or groups of people of various sizes, as well as organizations. A defamed person can be a politician that may have opposing views inside a country. In U.S. McCarthyism is tied to blame and half-truths or fabrication of nonsense of individuals that in any way object the state guidance to its citizenry. In Russia defaming has been used both internally and externally, for example to weaken politicians of European Parliament that have been publicly working against Russia and the Kremlin.

Defaming internally - to lower credibility and fame of a local politician, and the cause and leadership that specific individual presents. On some occasions, aftermath of defaming has caused assassinations or a disappearance of the defamed individual, where the defaming itself has served as a warning against one´s actions.

Defaming externally - to lower the credibility of a foreign individual; politician, corporate director or celebrity such a sportsman, to gain edge towards a larger cause of action, such as to have control over energy or media in a near-abroad country.

Deforming of Messages

The negative news can be turned into parties favor that change the meaning of the message. There can be a blend of aspects to the actual message so that reader and a follower of the specific event or news item loses track. The level of falsified news adjustment of any adversarial messages, ranges from bending half-truths to facts with various officially sounding names and topics. For example, western media can sometimes refer Russian terrorist attacks to acts of rebels instead of terrorism, and the Russian media talks about rebels instead of terrorism depending on their aim and purpose of the message.

Deviation of Events

Deviation of events is constant change of events, and fabricated messages surrounding those events. This causes misunderstanding of an event by intent. An event has taken place, with a clear and solid story behind it. However, after some passes some party questions the solidity and adds perspectives such as doubt and an alternate story-line that is reasonably close and could have taken place in natural ways with reasonable probability. Such alternate delusional stories are often blended with conspiracy theories or plots that part of us want to hear. The constant flux of messages may range from friendly agreement of items suitable for friendly media gestures, to sudden outburst of denial and accusation of opponent of hostilities. The constant change and relentless waves of media flux cause common man to get tired of following the event and eventually losing track of 'who did what'.

Degrade of Moral

It is the aim of the sender of propaganda to degrade moral in the opposite camp. Propagandistic messages such as to "take a day off" during the Second World War, stated in a poster provide aims to degrade the moral of the allied powers.

Media Disruption

To ensure solid defensive measures against information warfare, field of media operators must be uncompromised, detached from centralized ownership and control, and nondiscriminatory towards political, judicial, religious, ethical and defense dimensions in society. Deceptive means are used to lead a group of people to believe that an idea or a story is something else than it actually is. In television deception can be used by placing a news reporter in front of crowds that are actually hired for the purpose. A demonstration can be staged by a hired group of people that can range from dozens to thousands. A riot can be setup by men with balaclavas and riot police trying to control them, then televising that to international distribution. Events such as these can also be the first step towards an escalating conflict that is actually fabricated and, in the beginning, had no real world connection or a need. Airports, traffic central stations of large cities, town halls can all be used for staged celebrity greetings, with signs and greeting cards to increase the credibility of the action. A limousine may pick up the person staged as a celebrity, or a radio show may offer one its listeners celebrity treatment that includes a full suite of details offering a full experience. People that are unaware of the event will fall fully into the scenery and believe that there is some celebrity being greeted, without having the interest to ask who the person is, and even if they did ask, the reply from greeters could be anything as no one knows all celebrities globally.

If a person is financially well off, and get caught on using drugs the media may state it is a scandal. But if one is poor, it's depicted as a crime, this depends on how people as perceived by the media and if there is an element of deception involved. An example of a deception can be optical or in the message itself, depending on the cause and need of the government intent. Politicians need credibility and the assumption of others that there is public support behind the person being presented by the media. This gives a candidate edge they need, and supporters to opponents, if needed, to cause some protest and a gentle and pre agreed showdown that looks as there may be people not liking the candidate. This can give the politician more depth in their say and higher grade of credibility and a sense of seriousness in their matters of presentation for the masses.

The slide towards a regional conflict can be ignited by deceptive crowds causing havoc and a riot. Then escalating towards someone getting shot, with a response of a possible shoot back situation and onwards to larger masses come into play, and eventually men without insignia from the aggressor's side to join the battle with heavy equipment with the intent to take over a section of land, to annex into adversary's side. Such events can also be staged to disrupt the political system and the whole of parliament itself.

Rejection of Facts

When the flight MH17, (Malaysian Airlines flight from Amsterdam to Kuala Lumpur) was shot down in July 17, 2014, Russia denied the event quickly claimed by western media that the shoot-down was of Russian creation. Even though facts have built up regards to the evidence of the missile being Russian made, neither party West or East have agreed of any part of the facts surrounding the story. It is likely that the BUK missile itself was delivered from Russia to Ukrainian side of the border, then operated by a small group of rebellious pro-separatists driving eastern Ukraine towards Russian rule, the fact remains the same on both sides, Russian state denies the claims of Russian state involvement, and western governments claim the evidence is clear towards Russian responsibility.

Depending on the view, both parties can be right or wrong, depending on the view, perspective, details of the event and eventually the hard truth behind events. The denial that used against claims gives the other party either to withdraw its claims or to build a case against the denial. Similar to flight KAL 007 (September 1, 1983 killing 246 people) that was shot down when it had passed the Sakhalin peninsula, Russia on its way from Anchorage, Alaska to Seoul, South-Korea, the Soviet Union first denied the event, then claimed it was a spy plane. With denial the adversary gets a protective armor of the event and related action, that then, the opponent needs to counterclaim with a set of evidence, that is often an arduous task and sometimes take decades to solve. In this case, the event backfired as large scale anti-Soviet sentiment, distributed by media in the West. There have also other similar events that have first caused a denial affect in the minds and reporting of the perpetrator, such as Iran Air civilian flight 655, that was shot down July 3, 1988 by missile from a U.S. navy guided missile cruiser, then offered message of regret from U.S. to the families perished in the tragedy. Iran created a stamp of the event to distribute victim's role of U.S. policy. Similar media tactics were used by issuing stamps during Vietnam war by the Ho Chi Minh government, and Iranian government in the event of the hostage crisis in 1979.

Reference:
Loosely based on State Council Information Office Issues "China's Military Strategy", Xinhua, 2015 May 26th.
China's Propaganda System: Institutions, Processes and Efficacy by David Shambaugh, The China Journal No. 57, Jan. 2007. Pp. 25-58 by Chicago Journals
University of Turku, American Study Group - Intelligence lectures.
FIIA - Seminar, Media Power in International Politics, Sep 10, 2015, Helsinki
Incoherent Empire by Michael Mann 2003
http://www.globalissues.org

Comparisons of deliberate airline shoot-downs

Stripped denial of facts. Blame comparison of a deliberate airline shoot-down 1988 and 2014.

Flight MH17

Date: July 17, 2014

Denial

"Ukraine bears responsibility, not Russia." Vladimir Putin - 2014.

Blame

"Putin directly responsible for the MH17 crash" U.S. Government – 2014.

Flight Iran air 655

Date: July 3, 1988

Denial

"I will never apologize for the United States, I don't care what the facts are." George Bush - 1988.

Blame

"Gross negligence and recklessness amounting to an international crime" – Government of Iran – 1988.

Conclusions of Tactics

Information society resonates tones-of-influence created by information operations, both the steady wave of implemented tactics and separate larger operations. Combined disinformation themes, tactical policies and exploitation, structural deceptive tactics create the strategic deception (1). In a theater of deception strategy concludes reaching a vision that begins the influence campaign of propagandistic theme. The intent for influence building is to reach a critical mass of support and approval, tempting battle of stories to win hearts and minds, of focus demographic quarter of citizenry, typically rating from the intellectual-analytical towards common man of blue collar profession, to gain positive support of the society as a whole (2). This depends of the country, or corporation, that is intended to be overcome of sender's influence attempt, and the level of corruption that the regime of recipient includes. Higher corruption correlates to lower ground of influence efforts, the higher integrity and sincerity of a society, the more difficult it is for sender to influence the leadership, or masses in general.

Weather the attempt of influence is built through wishful thinking, denial of horror, mirror imaging, and to believe the unbelievable (3). Can a country bomb those in need to move masses, in order build weapons of influence, or is this just unreal thinking? Can someone shoot down a commercial airliner, or enable bombing of a jet airliner, just gain influence in a specific region or dispute. Or maybe there is a need to confuse global audiences, by creating campaigns of deceit, by obfuscating events and their relations to another of influence elsewhere, for example changing border between Georgia and Russia, or transferring discourse of border wall in Texas to no wall of Arizona, when disputing about drug trafficking.

This may be difficult with popular culture, the contemporary etiquette, that supports features of subject such as humor, amusement and ridicule - to see in the hat of magician, to reveal that there is no real content of fact in claimed fact, and that it is not a fact in the first place but a bogus attempt of lure viewer into world of illusion. Without the fact deception is all the easier to achieve for sender's benefit.

As we are unaccustomed to 'dare to look in the hat of the magician', and the opposite to believe the unbelievable. We risk being taken off guard and re-claim our credibility with in collective approval of society (4). When we grasp the nature of our perception and vulnerable interpretation of reality, we realize the intend of the sensed of influence, to translate those vulnerabilities into tools that sender of deception can benefit from - the flow of low aggression influence of soft power.

Reference:
1. Incoherent Empire by Michael Mann 2003
2. Media principles: Killed by friendly fire in US infowar, Index On Censorship (2002)
3. Themes of Soviet Strategic Perception and Disinfomration by John Lenczowski, 1987 and 2006
4. http://www.globalissues.org/article/399/killed-by-friendly-fire-in-us-infowar

Time Decay of Influence

Vast amounts of information being distributed and created every second, most of events with influence creation decay over time in the eyes of the recipient. This creates a high level of noise - information that an individual finds irrelevant or of low interest. Long term visual experience to rise above everyday media noise, requires either exceptionally tragic events, or sometimes, positive events such as a royal wedding, to overcome the media noise. Any event, positive or negative, decays over time. Events transform form current events to past events, a fading memory in our minds, and eventually an event in history. Time decay eats the efficiency of an influence event, positive and negative. When Russian consulted and equipped rebels operating in Eastern Ukraine shot down the Malaysian Airlines flight MH17, there was international outcry and disapproval of the events. There were instant demands to segregate Russia from world stage, as the activity in social media revealed the perpetrators being Russian fueled rebels. When Putin's clan in Kremlin realized west is incapable of responding militarily towards Russian aggressions, the conflict escalated quickly towards fueling east Ukrainian operations with more heavy weapons.

Every media event in the news decays over time. People simply forget and apart themselves from negative news to a safe distance. In 1980's there was considerably less information in their air. People read newspapers, heard the news on radio and television, read magazines and saw movies and of of course listened to music. But there wasn't social media as a communication channel and opportunity to mashup any information with still or live imagery and add their own commentary, causing everyone to create news themselves. The constant creation of information and consuming has raised the noise level of general information delivery far higher than it was some decades ago. The events breaking the current day general media noise level need to be exceptionally high, and therefore dramatic. The MH17 flight shoot-down was such an event, reaching global coverage but only for some days then fading from top news around the world the second or fifth item on the news. In couple of weeks the event blended into general news, that a portion of people followed. Chaotic scenes of the World Trade Center in September 2001 rose above the media noise levels for years. At the time internet was present, but was not widely used as it is today. Social media did not exist, video imagery ended up in YouTube placing the scene within easy reach for anyone. The time decay in this global distributed event was exceptional and created a strong resistance to time decay that lasted over a decade (1).

When the Malaysian Airlines MH370 disappeared and eventually ended up in the Indian Ocean in Spring of 2014, the ticket sales were dropped by 30% as claimed by Chinese ticketing agencies but then recovered in following months as the information fatigue takes over the consumers and business purchasing tickets (1). In the era of rising information volume and related complexities, there is so much to digest that the human memory quickly reassesses itself to process new events that take place, and the events that happened months ago quickly pass one's memory. During the first Malaysia air disaster western flight companies saw their Twitter message volume rise and fill up with negativities account for over 80% of the message flow. The Twitter volumes stood up for only three days then settling and turning the negativities to positivity. Some five months later when Malaysian Airlines MH17 was blown out of the sky with a Russian built BUK missile, the public was reminded of the notoriety of the brand and this time the message peaked above the media noise breaking the time decay in the previous message. Because of that, the sales went down even further and the negative sentiment took down the business of the airline, leading to government bailout of its debts and restructuring of the company. The double disaster was cause of lengthened battle that the public mindset did not forgive.

Similar event happened in September 1983, when a Korean

Airlines KAL 007 flew from Anchorage, Alaska heading for Seoul, Korea (2). In that incident a Russian MIG-15 shot down the Boeing 747 after it had passed the Sakhalin Peninsula north of Japan. Back then there was no social media, but the global turmoil in broadcast television and newspapers was so intense that the airline was forced to eventually change its name from Korean Airlines to Korean Air. The decay over time was clear in both cases but in 1980's, before the age of social media, information volume was much lower than it is today. A single event was enough to cause drastic changes in the brand, whereas today airlines sustain crash news better.

Reference
1. Madson Pter M. Perils and Profits: A Reexamination of the Link Between Profitability and Safety in U.S. Aviation, Bringham Young University, 3rd March 2013. Successful Crisis Management in the Airline Industry, Barcelor Thesis: Anna Hansson, Tomas Vikström, 2011-01-05, Uppsala University
2. http://journal-neo.org/2014/07/21/kal-007-case-shows-parallels-with-malaysian-airlines-mh17/ and the Time, September 13, 1983 in the article.

Author's interpretation of 1983's personal media projectile.

Tempting World of Sound

Message and Character

Audio waves can deliver us messages that are not present in our constant observations of reality. Music conveys views and opinions of a society and predict circumstances and views of our lives, part of citizenry, or a vast corporate customer base.

The transparency of music and its invisible transportation through airwaves, providing unnoted, unconscious and insidious notions of sound, has long been and continues to be under strict monitoring and even censorship especially in autocratic countries. The three dimensional output and presentation of music provides efficient way for both beholders as well as opponents of power, to relay their *leitmotif,* (1) the leading message, into the minds of citizens as a recognizable audio landscape that keeps on playing with constant repetition of timeless or striking message. Therefore, one could argue, that music is an ongoing broadcast advert that becomes an advertorial of sorts, an ongoing memory-trace-of-a-melody also called an "ear-worm", that inextricably plays in our heads. Our brain itches to fill in gaps of the tone and songs rhythm in our auditory cortex that is triggered when we hear music. Playing part of a song to a listener and then stopping it, causes our brains to fill in the missing pieces, in a way to remind us of the whole audio message of a song or rhyme. As an example, if a punk band plays a song where there are repetitive rhymes, then placing a gap in the message, the listener fills in the gap with the message, therefore causing the listener to become the operator of the propagandistic message. The way we can relay a brand related message, by repetition and playing tunes with missing beats and lyrics allowing the listener to fill-in essential pieces of a brand visuals and audio logo or tunes. One of the first "audio logos" was the Warner Brother's cartoon Bugs Bunny, where the rabbit or its hunter, Elmer, says with a gelled voice "that's all folks..." at the very end of the cartoon's closing music. This plays a unique message quickly reminding the viewer, even if the person is not watching the broadcast, of the cartoons repetitive cycle being played daily or weekly. Viewer can also easily relate faces and costumes to musical presentation and special effects, such as *Darth Vader* and the heavy breathe in Star Wars (Lucas film 1977-) saga. This connects distinct leadership and individual characteristics. Voice and singing function as essential part of human identity, creating an instant acoustic silhouette of our identity, that is mimicked by artificial robots making them human like creatures in our minds. In motion picture, the audience can swiftly relate to the visual of constant two-tone quick paced tempo of music from movie Jaws (1975, Steven Spielberg, music John Williams), and relate to the visualization of cut teeth imagery of a shark, presenting the unavoidable approach of the man-eating monster that attacks without a warning. In the tune of THX audio, sometimes presented before start of a movie the audience is alerted and advised to silence, focus on what's coming up next and be lost in a moment of confusion before the viewers are surprised with a gigantic dinosaur, attack behind enemy lines, assault on street, or a field of flowers with safe sounds of nature.

Musical Spheres

Music can be divided into multiple spheres. *Music*, the affective experience of the actual assembled sets of sound that makes us tap our fingers or pedal our foot, creating the physical activity of dance, the musical kinesthetic (1). The *performance* of a band or an artist. The *audience* that reflects the message relayed from the artistic performance back to stage and again back to audience. Musical *scenery*, as location and people that the experience was consumed with for the first *time* or the millionth repetition with years and seasons that relate to those memories, for example the legendary rock event in Woodstock, the summer of 1969, and in a song, The Summer of '69, by Bryan Adams, released in 1984. The music videos that typically playback during the musical performance on smartphones, tablets and television, create a dream-like surreal and futuristic postmodern pop-aesthetics. Visuals entice the listener in an audiovisual flow-state and the visualization of harmonic chord effects presented content intertextually.

Immersive Reality

Sounds and music of video games have grown into an industry of their own, being a mixture of graphical and emotional narrative that blend into an immersion of the player and the instant virtual-reality of the game. Audio world in games is different from motion picture, as games have an interactive and adaptive sound repertoire that reacts to player's actions in the game, causing the experience never being identical to earlier gaming sessions. Games have wide blanket coverage in specific age groups and geographic areas. With tens of millions of players games provide an audience that can be affected with audio and visual messages. These elements are presented in the game internal vicinity and also in the actual gaming characters active in the story narrative. The gaming platforms have offered both commercial and political influence opportunities for since 1970's. Missile Command (Atari

1980) presents a scenario where western cities are attacked with an endless hail of ballistic missiles presenting player as a regional commander of multiple anti-missile batteries guarding cities from being destroyed. Some games have proven such strong influence in our society that there has been legal debate and debacle over their legality. Grand Theft Auto (Rockstar Games, 1997) is an action adventure game where the set is located in fictional American cities, that present American urban surroundings such as Miami area, Greater New York metro-area and California. Even though the game series contains humor and satire there is controversy over games adult oriented characters and related narratives, operating in a criminal underworld with beatings, role playing, street racing and third-person shootings overall presenting a violent theme. Such games have questionable imagery. Legal action against intends to prove to inspire players to commit shootings (Hamel, Bede, 2003) based on games "purported psychological effects, ideas and concepts". Because of such content, the gaming series is now-a-days being split into multiple universes and has increased its massive financial success. Multiplayer gaming platforms such as World-of-Tanks present historic and modern-day battles where thousands of players replay battles of World War II. Some of the groups are fanatic, waking up in the middle of the night depending on their physical time zone. They participate in a combat activity of virtual reality that strains their ties in real-world.

Audio and Lyrical Fill-in

Spreading influence, in a society as well as relaying a favorable message to customers of a corporation, through music and audio messages that stay in the minds of people for days or decades, are strong enough to overthrow even governments or to grab market share from a weakened competitor. In mythologies and the Bible, sound has incredible powers, as sound of a trombone destroys walls of Jericho and informs its listeners of the doomsday. An example of the repetitive power of a message can be presented as follows; When the song "Old McDonald had a farm" is repeated multiple times in a verse of an audio broadcast, then play-backed as "Old McDonald had a..", our brain fills in the word "farm" into the lyrics. In this simplified example where the message is part from a children's song, the well-known lyrics are filled in fraction of a second, and similarly the message could be from a politically motivated song, a sports event like Olympics, World Championships or even a song about crime. Few of us know the Olympic theme, but many remember the year and location when we hear sound of a specific commentator relating to a sports event, such as the finals of a 100-meter-dash.

In Finland, the nation as a whole knows the Swedish wording "Den glider in", translates loosely as "it slides in" referring to hockey puck gliding to a goal past a goalie, as that was the hockey tune from 1995 World Championships that Finland won over Sweden. Events in sports and related tunes, partly helped to push the country out of economic crisis of the time. If the previously mentioned "Den glider in" example tone is played anywhere in Finland in part "Den glider...", practically everyone knows how the rhyme goes filling missing pieces, unconsciously, with their brains.

Contradictory Influence

Sound has multiple effects in a multi-dimensional world of lyrics and rhythm, tone and audio visual presentation of vocals. Music, a compilation of tones, tempo, lyrics and rhythm of audio, has proven to be an efficient way to disseminate one's ideas, such as Bruce Springsteen's song Born in the U.S.A. (Columbia, 1984) was presented during the Cold War of the 1980's. When rapper Brandon Duncan wrote lyrics to his songs he went rather unnoticed for over a decade. But then the San Diego law enforcement became interested of this rap songs, connected the lyrics to earlier shootings committed by other people, and Mr. Duncan was charged with "gang conspiracy" (3). He never shot anyone, but the link towards gang violence by making music, caused the rap artist being of accused of crimes one had not committed, but had written songs about. The provocative punk rock band Pussy Riot presented offensive music in 2012, in performances that stage unauthorized guerrilla performances with a feministic theme and a vocal opposition to Russian President Vladimir Putin, who is seen as a dictator in the band's musical narrative. Eventually poking the beehive of Kremlin with anti-leader performances ended band's live performances in Russia with charges of hooliganism and an 18-month prison sentence (2).

In extreme cases audio has been used as a method of torture, for example in war operations of the 9/11 aftermath in Iraq, where Iraqi prisoners were forced to listen to high volume music repeatedly in a "disco room" without the ability to remove the headset from oneself.

Conclusions of Sound

Regards to sounds and audio, motion and video, everything from *speech singing* a.k.a. rap-music to performances at the opera to midi-ringtones of early mobile phones. Whether the content is a poem with self-created tone-of-character or high speed chase in motion picture, one can argue that the experience of sound is a combination of voice, lyrics, tempo, verse, but also visuals in still and motion picture. In a musical narrative, all this binds together in repetitive appearances in persons imagery through eyes, reverberation in ears, audio-vibrate-imagery on skin, becoming an overall musical experience.

Listeners and viewer's personal life-experience, time of day, weekday, moon phase, season and location where the experience took place, as well as one's personal history and background, create the overall character of influence that eventually binds all the input from human senses together (4). After all, we as humans consume the environment into our bodies that function as an *integrated-psycho-physical-structure*.

References:
1. Taide, kokemus ja maailma - Risteyksiä tieteidenväliseen taiteidentutkimukseen. Toim. Yrjö Heinonen, 2014 p. 22, 24-26, 29, 57.
2. Wikipedia: Pussy Riot, Missile Command arcade game, Grand Theft Auto video game.
3. Article: When Rap Music is a Crime, The Atlantic, by Karlanna Lewis, March 7th, 2015.
4. University of Turku, U.S. Studies Group lectures, January - March 2015.

7. Superpowers in The Making

Terrorism, Phases and Media

Counter terrorism and the related battle intertwine United States, Russia and China into a partnership that neither of them wants to be in, but are forced into, each with their own motives. The ongoing information war, resources, tactics, means and goals, are operational particles that we see on a daily basis in our media sphere. All this opens and fluctuates the relations with the powers, as these nation states share some of their knowledge while hiding the other half. America and Europe share the views to shut-down terrorist funding and the need to the close distribution of the ideology of violence spread through social networks. It is a challenge to allow and limit technical capabilities for everyone's access but only for peaceful content. Russia sees counter-terrorism as information to benefit from. It is distributed through state-owned media outlets. Content distribution, cultural, artistic and educational operators can provide wide coverage for their messaging. The counter message needs to be opposing terroristic propaganda, racist ideologies and religious intolerance. Russia sees that United Nations are the main driver to enforce action on an international scale. Terrorism is seen as a product of a unipolar world created by the United States as the country had no counter force for over two decades.

Russia proposes that America has created a global sphere, or rather, a dome, of negligent world politics with experimental aspects.

Terrorism Development Phase	(years)
Anarchistic	1870-1910
Nationalistic	1920-1960
Neo leftist	1960-1980
Religious	1970-2020 (1)

In the latest variant of terrorism, the essential areas are suicidal bombings that are mashed into various technology innovations. The targets range from America to Israel, European nations to Russia and Middle-East and its secular Muslim populations. Origins for religious terror are born out of Soviet military presence in Afghanistan and resulting war, and the overthrow of the Shaw in Iran in 1979.

Modern terrorism disintegrates the societies social cohesion by removing the feeling of security. From streets to bedrooms, militants intend to expand their power by serving threats through the imagination of its victims (4). While at the same time, terrorism and its message, through on-demand video, television broadcast and social media seeks to weaken the values western world believes in, the validity of Western Saga; family, peace, well-being and high quality of life. Therefore, terrorism is a part of psychological warfare, a system of international crime projected in sophisticated ways (2). Terrorism challenges our understanding the traditional defence of societies and the battle of fronts by acting in the asymmetric model, and creating a mash-up and fluctuation of information warfare and psychological play. ISIS has spread the message through Twitter, 'our violence will terminate in your bedrooms.' a messaging tactic to deliver horror and fear in target audiences minds.

Terrorism is a blend of guerrilla warfare and its surprising functionality (3), by evaluating its weaknesses and divisiveness, propagandistic reflections and the distribution, that modifies and frameworks the messaging in such fashion that its fits into the modern way of communication, social media, especially Twitter and YouTube, that are used both for message relay for broad coverage of audiences and recruitment of new warriors. As in mass persuasion, the terroristic messaging uses all available methods and tactics to disseminate its message, as its rhetoric's and message are fit to be carried by any media; radio, on-demand and broadcast television, newspapers, magazines, blogs, web pages, tweets, imagery fitting into social media with reporters and bloggers as actuators. This media-oriented terrorism aims to pressure our leaders and influencers, politicians and secretaries, and to submit themselves to the political demands presented by terrorists, similar to artists of sarcastic cartoons presented according to western freedom of speech in a democracy are pressured to cease their operations and therefore to carry their purposes over other priorities. This is fairly easy in western societies as all production and consumption of information is mainly free and without restrictions (2).

Systematically planned operations of WTC 9/11/2001 strikes reflected an attack against traditional values, wealth and commercial well-being of the West. The symbolic facts strike hearts and minds, as the terrorist system of beliefs bases itself on, message-public-fear-change model. The systemic model can be thought to consist of four components; sender, recipient, message and feedback, and in terrorism the components are; terrorist, victim, bomb, reaction. The systemic model is simple and easily repetitive, therefore, one can say that terrorism is scalable and a volume business. The repetitive function is amplified by social media. The physical action is used to support the propaganda agenda. Terrorists use psychological warfare (PSYOP) (1), to recruit of new participants, activate global networking, and guide targeted propaganda. Recruits are aimed by messaging, geographic focus and the glamour and glory of the life as a member of a terrorist group. This has similarities to pop idol fanatics that worship their target and glorify the lifestyle and output that it produces. Cells function as groupies to the centered control of actions, the idol. Assassinations of opponent military personnel serve as the means to justify actions that terrorist have performed. Use of violence and attached rhetoric amplify use of rampage in various ways. The asymmetric attacker has capability to implement its warfare to render defender's traditional capabilities insufficient. Decapitating the idol, will create stories of legend, while lessening instant benefit of the campaign.

Reference:

1. Berger Heidi, Venäjän Informaatio-psykologinen sodankäyntitapa (in Finnish), 2010
2. Seminar: FIIA - Media Power in International Politics, Sept. 10, 2015, Helsinki
3. Seminar: FIIA – Power Transformation, Sept. 9 2015, Helsinki
4. The Atlantic 03/2015, What ISIS Really Wants?

Glorification of a Terroristic Message

Al-Qaeda's ultimate goal is to reinvigorate the Islamic umma in a confrontation with the West. Then mobilize the revolutionary movement against the democratic countries. Al-Qaeda's media strategy aims ultimately at a fundamental restructuring of the political identity of the Islamic world, with a discourse presenting all of the Muslim world causing a multitude of opinions and views of participation. The jihadists have found the Arab media at least in part unreliable, quoting "The media people who belittle religious duties such as jihad are atheists and renegades" a quote by Osama Bin Laden in January 2004. The Arabic media gave rounded quotes of the London 7th 2005 terrorist attacks, while hotel bombing attacks in Amman, Jordanian were condemned strictly throughout the region. The use of internet through discussion boards, e-mail, videos, encrypted intent messaging and literature with high-quality magazines, are aimed for western audiences to gain access to the first stage in self-radicalization process. Governments must ensure there is the delivery of information for Westerners to identify and report such information and the related steps taken and the warning signs in the process of self-radicalization. When individuals are well informed by the western media, the understanding of identifying individuals before they fall into prey of terrorist illusive media is essential.

Terrorism functions as a microcosm of the complexities of our society, facing a civilized model and indoctrinating it with savage that creates a fear effect in Westerners, causing our societies to fragment and divide – making us afraid in our bedrooms. If this is the intention then it is essential that the media we see informs us of the model and the intentions, with a constant flow of information in a relentless force of waves so that the message will penetrate us as audiences to counter the terrorist acts with reasonable thinking. ISIS messaging through a variety of media channels and raw content is full of nihilism and absurdity and filled with symbolic messages. ISIS has brought a multitude of external narratives in explosive ways into our minds, as a house of mirrors, concaves and asymmetric. Absolutism, history, political determinism is characterised by these explosive narratives, where all of this reflects a timeless historical rebelliousness. The savagery of terrorism represents out-of-group items as objects of the group attacks on, with revenge. It has been said that ISIS has six pillars or fathers it stands on; occupation, despotism, sectarian aggressiveness, Gulf Salafism, historical puritanism, and violence - differences and similarities oppose the inequitable globalisation that capitalism as western democracies represents, to them, the wrongful world order. ISIS has been created in Iraq and the Levant's home of the two caliphates and the environment of two Ba'athist regimes, one leftist and one rightist, the environment has been then enforced by British colonialism and Ba'athist despotism, with an aftermath of United States occupation, followed by sectarian oppression.

Unfortunately, these are groups of people that are willing to do anything it takes, to vandalize and break away from the rather stable but often financially and economically tough environment that our expanding income gap widens. Terrorists exploit the openness of western democracies, Russian autocracy, and China's one party for all models, all of these systems functioning in a capitalistic model, in their own right. The terrorist groups often built by bullied males raised in the west and holding local passports, fall into the media trap created as an illusion, a scenery of a mirage, life that does not exist. The Jihadist networks operate advanced systems to have their vision above the media noise for everyone's eyes and ears. Terrorist groups originating from Sahel countries in Africa, Syria, Sudan, Yemen, and other countries where either part of whole of the state has failed in its activity to framework the society in such manner that people are able to masses to educate and employ themselves without the frustration and tempting opportunism joining a terrorist organization, are presented by a well-run media organizations with constant publishing of motion and still imagery as well as magazines depicting a life that is presented as glamour and glory being bogus. Many of the people running the terrorist media outlets are highly educated in top western run institutions such as Colleges and Universities in the United Kingdom and France.

While al-Qaeda's media strategy has been based on careful centralized media control, the visuals are created by spectacular attacks gaining maximal media exposure, mashed with carefully times video message of Osama Bin Laden prior to U.S. raid on Abbottabad in Pakistan, being the terrorism phenomenon of the 2000's. When the western security services woke up the realm of al-Qaeda's capabilities they eventually managed to gain control of the terrorist penetration into busses, trains and plains, every part of a western cityscape. This caused al-Qaeda's capacity to fade and gave more creative and social media fancy ISIS to take over. The spectacular media events of al-Qaeda that were driven by a visual scenery of "older men in caves" metamorphosed into social media driven glamour and idolised model of ISIS that understood the need to rise above the noise in social media. Then spreading into local neighbourhood boys and girl in their teens, advising them for a nominal cause but in such manner that it looks tempting, hedonistic and materialistic at the same time packaged with a twisted combination of sex, bikini's, sports cars and bloody revenge.

The *digihad* of Islamic world will continue, manufacturing content that is high quality, video game like, extremely rough in its visuals, but at the same time create a sea of tranquility to provide higher credibility and calm of mindset for its followers, children eating chocolate, men fishing in sun, heads chopped off on the third image to cause a wake-up call, and bind to the wars of ideas. Information age weapons of media are shaped by their type and velocity of the information delivery, such as Twitter with the recruit, manage, motivation and executive order provided in seconds globally. Related tactics include Twitter rented accounts and hijacked hashtags. It is common that the medium delivery provider, that receives a message from terrorist organisations media section, provides the information through rented Twitter accounts, where they have direct control to publish into tens of thousands of accounts directly. This is done by middleware that the jihadist sympathiser has installed to their PC or MAC, and the application opens up the passage to each of these people social media accounts, therefore leaving voluntarily the access totally in the hands of the terrorist organisations media centre. And when there is a major event in the world, such as Olympics or World Cup football (soccer) competition, the terrorist media organizations, such as the Al-Hayat Media Center, the foreign language media division of the Islamic State, push out messages in great scale to have massive volumes of messages and therefore making their message above the media noise in social networks. All these pieces of tactical operations tie into a systemic way to operate towards a strategic target, domination of media. Jihadist media centres abuse trending topics to rise above other news, they plan and recruit also on Facebook, then commence plans and attacks on Twitter and create a visual scenery that reports their atrocities on YouTube. At the same time, the field of information persuasion has medium pace information such as major news organisations such as CNN and BCC. The slow page information is longer term and has more of a lifestyle aspect in its influence. Such lifestyle propaganda, for example, is the jihadist magazine Inspire. Imagery that at the same time creates a perspective of children eating chocolate and people being hanged, while riding a super sports car in the evening with ladies. These glamour images are weapons of media manipulation for potential terrorist recruits, sweetened with capitation images as to project power flow into the often bullied reader, who sees a pop idols imagery in the terrorist leaders. All this is an opening in life, to join a team that looks winning, glamour filled and wealthy, something that one can participate at will and depart after the appetite of revenge towards the west is done. However, after arrival the facade falls and the horrors of war kick in, pushing away the glorified glamour that sucked in the victim that turned into a terrorist, a metaphysical fighter, all this created by the digital of today.

The synthetic terrorist created a glamourized message is topped with hate, activates fear and anger in young males, envy with primal response to the anti-American way of life. Muslims in America and Muslims in middle-east live a completely different life, and the, therefore, a motion picture that depicts western values is unable to make an emotional impact on the primal emotions of Jihadist prone viewers. The terroristic media presentation is about anger, cultivated with glitter and a hunt-to-kill-game-like illustration, without mental connection, that delivers a discourse of a pop-idol-like-life, fighting for a cause blended with revenge of a life that was unreal and unachievable for its viewer. Both, ISIS and Al Qaeda, confirm and grip into a clash-of-civilization narrative, that has helped with a disintegrated social demographics of some European societies to turn into a jihadist seedbed and breeding ground, transposing its recruitments frustration and purposeless itinerancy, from failed states of Sahel, the Northern Africa, to the classy narratives of sport cars and luxury of the western desires. Terrorists sacrifice human lives, West limits human casualties and sacrifices spending, budget allotments that enable the use of technology. The party that sacrifices most will eventually conquer the war.

Reference:

Left Catholicism 1943-1955: Catholics and Society in Western Europe at the Point of Liberation
New York Times 2015/12/13
THE EVOLUTION OF STRATEGIC INFLUENCE by LTC SUSAN L. GOUGH UNITED STATES ARMY
Startup Africa by Sami Leino (Chapter, Terrorism).

Russian Media-Machine

After 2012 it started to become clear, the Russian leadership consists of a group of men that befriended and studied in 1970's and 1980's KGB run schooling in St. Petersburg and Moscow. They knew each other well, could trust their inner circle to an extent, and were rebuilding the Russian sphere of influence through massive investments for a systematically built news organisation. The media system in the works would disseminate their view of the world as the Kremlin would see proper and suitable regards to their intentions, to regain reverence and stature in the world. After all, what one says in a news broadcast, is at least up to a point, presented as a fact for its viewers and a business decision of the news organisation. The people that are running Russia, have suffered from a post-traumatic disorder of past Soviet times, but the wealth, win and conquest of the Russian 1990's wild years had made them greedy for power.

The typical characteristics of Russian society are a rough way to enforce the use of interests, the ruthless battle of internal groups, a blurred line of illegal and legal operations, degrading capability and value of judicial authorities, corruption in its widest meaning and country wide scale. Vladimir Putin on has created a step by step proceeding tight system of fierce grip, where most border siding areas such as organised crime and sidelining activity have been taken as a tool for authorities to hammer with. Russian influence operations and the overall doctrines have no place for the truth of facts, no lines of good taste, the intent is to deceit, deny, distort messages and to defame decision-makers, and to eventually surprise attack the enemy. West may see the battle of medias in a state of truce, in a sea of tranquillity, but in fact, Russian media wars are in constant operations and tactical use, that we do not see, until the attempt to divide and conquer, are further with gained advance in operations. Russia sees that West portraits Russia negatively, so what would change. West and East live in separate realities, the Russian leadership is about showing strength in the face of own people, without any relevance what Western governments of citizenry presents as their thoughts, it does not matter in Russia, western specialists amaze themselves wondering how Russian Prime minister can deny clear facts and lie. This ensures the Kremlin to stay in power and relives the war that was lost but only temporarily, and this time to win it.

The setbacks in international politics that Russia experienced during 2014-2015, have resulted in an activity militarily and politically. The leadership switched to a mode of crisis, catastrophic and hysteria that was created by the media department of the Kremlin and distributed by state-controlled television. This has included the creation of imagery that purports enemy images, victimisation, isolation as Russia is viewed as a fortress. The ways engagement is done by aggressive use of broadcast media has increased the resilience of the regime, but the main problems in the society remain unsolved. The Russian system is built on unofficial networks of power, relations and control that systematically enforces the rulers but limits the reforms, and therefore, long-term problems remain unsolved. The hysteria mode, that the Russia system is in, instrumentalized and legitimises its power that society faces resulting in loss of quality of living in the longer term, that goes through the society for a longer period. Therefore, the hard times are pushed systematically onwards, and they will step-by-step become worse, instead of dealing and solving them. Isolationistic, passive, populist means are tools that the Russian leaders use as tools eliminate alternative options for the country and at the same time enable the Kremlin to hold on to its power.

Russia will remain a high-risk state with its economy, infrastructure, politics, judiciary, degrade of Rubble, and international agreements and pacts, until foreseeable future. The falling energy and increasing presence of NATO and EU all create friction in the post-Soviet sphere that Russia is competing from, while the cause-or-consequences relation, result in the prolonged economic downturn in an environment of undiversified economic structures. Some alternation in matters happen by themselves due to internal constant degrade, a cause of Kremlins actions and due to external pressure from sanctions – all this creating a vicious circle that the country finds even more difficult out-spiral itself from. All makes governance complex and unpredictable, but present Putin as the personification of hopes, even though the system is larger than the president and therefore in slow motion that fights in inertial means with forces that both pull the country into disintegration as in early 1990's, but also into deeper autocracy and centralized power, similar to Soviet era. People trust the president above all, but there are fractures between president and authorities in the country itself. Also, it is important to note that people in general trust the "governance of Russia" meaning Putin, but lag in their trust towards regional and especially local authorities, the system. This creates a great risk in the dictatorship that the country is quickly approaching, if the leader goes, the system may falter. Russia tested the succession from Putin to Medvedev with his presidency, but Medvedev was unable to acquire the 'above nation' and a 'hope for future' status.

In Russian leadership vision, having a strong state guided news organization with western standards is one of their key pillars of power for the 2020's. The Russian leadership has put the progress and reforms out the window, cooperation and diplomacy that were mutually invested in Russia, European Union and America were lost when Russia invaded Crimea, values and beliefs that the Kremlin built in the beginning of the millennium have been nullified. These have been switched to enforcing national security with limiting freedom of the press, the legal framework of justice in society and the direct repressive internal power from state to the citizenry, by taking into tight control the overall property including all mineral resources of the nation state. A second thesis we can see is the strengthening domestic security with Soviet-era control, suppression and snooping system regards to all communications at the same time wiping out anything that even remotely presents a theoretic distant counter force to the regime in power. Therefore, any political reforms as distant and unlikely. In Russia, these tools are used while at full throttle, while at the same time; the blame game is a pointing finger towards anything West, such as lagging nationwide purchasing power and mass layoffs in some areas spreading further across the vast nation. Russia confronts challenges with Putin's doctrine – a militaristic confrontation that offences a belligerent and offensive nation with a 'one-hour readiness from barracks to positions.' Regards to hard power, Russia's emerging doctrine of so-called hybrid warfare, it is increasingly using a mix of conventional force, Special Operations mission and new weapons in the 21st-century battlefield. This involves the use of space, cyber, information warfare and hybrid warfare designed to cripple the decision-making cycle of the alliance. The Kremlin's opportunistically seeks to benefit from internal crisis situations to enforce its power and fight the domestic political apathy, as a conclusion one could say that the main driver for Russia is 'suicidal statecraft'.

Rebuilding Russian Sphere

The toolbox of Russian president includes a variety of extension power in practical form. Organization and people close to criminal activities are held close, such as the Night Wolfs where classic national socialistic values are prevalent, as the organisation have distanced itself from Western counterparts such as the US originating Hells Angels. The political aspects have risen in recent times over inter-gang activities and cooperation, which again has risen tensions between the criminal groups. The Kremlin uses night Wolfs as a tool to strengthen and guideline the decision made, both internally and outside Russian borders. The orientation is to keep a strong grip of nationalism and push that with a momentum towards outward pointing threats such as efforts to disintegrate Russia. The criminal organisations of multiple kinds have therefore a shield of operations from the Kremlin as long as they strongly support the guidance given by the president and "thwart" outside efforts to pull Russia apart.

These pinpoint operations have been decided in the Kremlin for areas that were part of former the Soviet Union, and especially the Baltic states, or parts of them. Russian-speaking minorities see these semi-criminal organisations such as Night Wolfs as their heroes and supportive "comrades from Mother Russia." Russian way to build a wide range of tools to rebuild their sphere of influence ranges from TV channels to local news websites, blended with operative forces such as motorcycle clubs, bloggers and trolls who insert Pro-Russian comments in native languages.

All this is part of an asymmetric hybrid warfare, as a militia that can be legally sent abroad to plan, execute, report and pull-back to Russia for safety, for any tactical operation as a part of the long-term strategic plan to serve Russian interest and rebuild the sphere of influence outside Russia's borders. Russian broadcast domestic television and the global Russian media are media tools of the state to operate the society control and mass persuasion techniques to create a narrative to overrun any western worldview. Seemingly, to legitimise the Russian non-existent truth model and view of matters that turn half-truths into a simplified full truth. This can be achieved by any method from defaming an influential politician near abroad, to denial of events and facts other nations broadcast. Constant reroute of events, aims as to keeping up the flux is done to obfuscate the overall narrative, so that the one's keeping up will have at least some confusion to understanding details of events, chronological timeline, with an ever increasing intensified tempo. The aim for Russian media is to neutralise and reverse any western accusation that is made against the Kremlin.

Troll farming has proved one model in spreading false commentary and sentiment in the media. These propagandists can be seen as information warfare terrorists that initiate the tactics of operations. In practice, this is done by employing individuals who are paid between $500 to $3000 per month for saturating news sites and commenting polls with pro-Russian sentiment and made up 'facts' that often turnaround the fact of the story into an alternative view that is actually a half-truth leaving out the essence of the message, or to a total nonsense that intends to confuse the reader. This creates a pro-Kremlin populist view of any local or foreign issue, discrediting Western views and intending to make a factual message bogus. Kremlin is going to a full media war blended with medium and hard power, assaults and physical violence, a hybrid warfare that adjusts the flame of war accordingly. Russia tries to build an atmosphere where Russians can feel they no longer are humiliated. The main methods for Russian media are to defame and discredit politics and political institutions in the west, plant stories and create defamatory content aiming to discredit people and organisations on country, nation and city and to enforce pro -Russian compatriot groups and extremists of all sorts.

Russian media broadcast channels are a continuous weapon, in use nonstop around the clock portraying its campaigns against the West, with the intention that facts are what the news channels disseminate. The country has learned from the grave mistakes it made losing the media propaganda war in 1980's. Now it has taken a solid stance and rigorous method with huge capital expenditures on how to run pro-Russian information warfare against the West, or anyone opposing its interests and belligerency, challenging Western governments with an asymmetric media warfare. Russia is adjusting, testing and combining media influence with physical assault and evaluating how strong the media influence is and how much leverage it can bring for larger scale overall advancement against Western politicians and influencers. The Russian media will use increasingly egregious methods in extending its sphere of influence anywhere, especially in Europe and partially against the United States, that is seen as the eventual enemy. The media warfare is a toolset to fill-in the actual adversarial efforts in weakening the West, in general, and the European states. In 1980's the United States presented covered propaganda in television and movies, there is an alternative offered by the east and the West needs to bring in their assortment of media persuasion in the competition of a global media presence. Modern Russia sees the Gerasimov doctrine as essential ways to build influence through, non-militarized method, a mainframe of today's warfare. Because Information society resonates tones-of-influence created by informational operations, both the steady wave of implemented tactics and separate larger operations. Russia prioritises the noninvasive means as the cost-efficient method to combat constant waves of information wars, in relentless waves of operations, that support other means of warfare when needed. The information battle softens adversary's society to accept pro-Russian thoughts and values, and in optimal operation there is no need to fire a single bullet, or at least all battle operations are minimised as was seen in the invasion of Crimea.

Putin's regime may have calculated, that Russia as a nation may not be able to keep up with the West and Asia without the Kremlin taking considerable power chokehold on Russia's resources. It is possible, that Russia is unable to rise, but will break into a multitude of smaller nations splitting the wealth of natural resources more evenly. The Kremlin has seen, likely with an erroneous calculus, that the only way to succeed is to run Russia as a dictatorship, building as a resource pool for their own good and vision. That vision is hosted in minds of people in their sixties who fantasise the old Andropov era strength of 1984. That dream isn't coming back, but that does not block from nationalistically romanticising about it. The international cooperative with a balance of West and East lives is going through a longer period of imbalance and outright hostilities, this is a challenge for the United States either to lead as the bright star of freedom or to take the third seat of the waggon after China and Russia. Europe with its non-united states of Europe will remain a casket of states some belonging to NATO, some to European Monetary Union and some to the European Union all rowing on the same boat with incoherent pace.

Influencing people, organisations and nations by slowing down specific solutions and creating objects to delay an obvious outcome are tactical tools to reach a positive outcome, sometimes to simply limit losses or to delay the unwelcome outcome. Conflicts that Russia creates in its near borders are tailor-made and suited for various purposes. They are a toolset that can be quickly adapted and slightly tailored to fit a specific time and geopolitical instance to reach a favourable outcome. History has shown that politicians who have been elected to parliament for their primary season have a certain weakness and this perspective; they can be influenced easier than seasoned masters who have held the grip of power for years. In a way Russia uses the same methods West used in the 1980's; the east uses strong media-agitation and modifying media, whereas today's' West's positive themes are laudable causes, traits and acts.

The essential piece of Russian intentions to undress the credibility of Western leaders, receive the support of its citizens - home and abroad, and recreate a favorable Russian group of people for its support, and at the same time have a peek into decision making in each of Western countries and receive notification of intended results before they are implemented to create a response in beforehand to thwart any unfavorable action. This is done both in direct diplomatic channels but also publicly as to present the situation in the eye of the beholder and present manufactured truths to support choices made against politicians and their decisions, with a frameset that only has favorable options for the presenter. For example, the Russian sanctions have been valued with a variety of tone in different European countries. Some countries refrain participating in sanctions due to economic reverberations. Media creates tempting messages that court audiences towards attempt of sanctions. Broadcast media, bloggers, radio stations and trolls all fight a constant battle to hold the integrity of facts and as a counter message to disintegrate and deny the message, then to create an engram that is favorable for one's side. The mental image, conception are one of the most important hunches in today media tactics and related counter-acts of information. The soft power of media, plays one important part in Russian major intentions; to have have Europe under its foot, disintegrated, and at the same time have the resource of America being dispersed with China, Russia and India, aiming to cause more weight for east than West, and break NATO with momentum of mass. The West needs sustainability and perseverance, budgets and collaboration, to react to Russian lead campaigns of tailor truths.

In our times, the world order is complex and multifaceted with interconnected links in multiple dimensions and dependencies, the influence can be built for a common man by offering them a simplified truth with two choices, an easy but limited offering. The populist parties in various European countries have proven that this model works, as has Donald Trump in his Presidential election campaign in the U.S. where the solution has typically presented as himself. Trump and Putin have competing functionalities in their presentation and leadership, but they also have some common ground as they both promise to save their country from external threats and return the greatness of their countries. During this debate, China has begun to create their variant of a superpower to replace both Cold War era powers with China's version of hard, medium and soft power.

References (Russian Mediasphere and Russian Media-Machine):

FIIA analysis, December 2015, Zugzwang in slow motion?
Belarus Digest 25th July 2011 - Choking the Social Networks Revolution
Obama's Foreign Policy Fiia Briefing Paper - October 2015
Users of social media in Belarus - Mikhail Doroshevich
Russian Protest On and Offline Briefing Paper February 2012 fiia.fi
No Change on The Horizon Briefing Paper September 2015 fiia.fi
Switching to digital: Presidential elections in Belarus blogs.fco.gov.uk
The Economist May 23rd 2015, Aug 23rd 2007
FIIA Crafting the EU Global Strategy 2015
Ulkopolitiikka magazine 1/2015
FIIA.fi Media Power In International Politics, September 10, 2015
University of Turku, American Study Group classes January -March 2015

8. Conclusions

Proliferated Media Capabilities

The abundance of information that was earlier available only to top statesman level, is today available for everyone. From satellite images to message encryption of all sorts, we mostly access knowledge through Google. The former technological edge that the West had, has narrowed. Related technology know-how has proliferated and therefore lost its meaning in the competition of geopolitical blocs of power. Reflections to people's minds are immediately baked into masses of social media, honoring no boundaries of states.

This causes millions of people to have access to resources, never before available, to anyone with a smartphone in their pocket, in any state in the world. This will accelerate the rise of knowledge and growth of economies, wealth, personal independence but also volatility with people, markets and societies, but at the same time, this increases hostilities and personal knowledge beyond the world of order from heads of state, causing security challenges for third world countries. Think of a drone, delivering meals to every door in minutes around a city, or a chemical weapon payload, a toxic menace, around city's downtown during the rush hour. The challenge is how to eliminate such a small flying thing instantly, and in the broader picture, how to solve the complex problems arising from masses of information having wanted and unwanted data items, the paradox stands with all industries, individuals and intelligence equally. Identity theft, change of information on people's screens they endlessly trust by hacking into and altering the services people use, such as banking, create challenges that are exploited by organized crime networks operating globally. Some of us criticize the drone age and its risks to the society we live, while others claim that the same people could shoot at trucks driving on a motorway.

It took companies like Starwood Hotels to grow to the plus ten billion market capital company four decades, since the early

1980s. It took Airbnb to gain a valuation of twenty billion in less than seven years. The future pace of value creation will grow even quicker into trillions of dollars in market valuations. Future companies will grow in months and out innovate veteran market operators in weeks. Only 60% of Fortune Top companies will exist in ten years' time, and that prediction moves forward daily as we wake up every morning, meaning that the era of instant outsiders in the world is not going away or stopping but constantly accelerating in its pace and complexity, being interconnected to multiple facets in our societies, causing us being interdependent between nation-states as well as corporations across borders, both economic and political. Changes become rapid, the pace of innovation and product delivery execution accelerates exponentially, therefore upbringing new products, services and companies in months, even weeks, rather than years.

As a species we, humans, evolve much slower into next phase. But in time, we do cope better with an abundance of information that increasingly is poured into our brains. We adapt to the current information fatigue by processing more information, refining some of that into knowledge, but at the same time our level of tolerance towards fresh news will rise, and the recognition of events will note only greater changes in information alteration than before. The level of noise increases and so does our contrast of the differentiation from normal. Therefore, shocking news of today, will not be shocking a decade from now. People will only respond to even more extreme events and stories.

Some of the Forbes 500 companies that feel currently secure, reluctant to progress will face sudden challenges by newcomers on their markets, digitizing quickly their fully or semi-analogues businesses, they don't see what's coming up, as these institutions are at a standstill without realizing that themselves. For example, banks in early 1990's and during the 2008 financial meltdown aftermath felt, that by doing nothing, one can evade risk, which eventually disrupted most of the banks forcing them to merge or to be taken to government control. The 'do nothing to save a company' thinking, equals to 'do nothing wrong' is the equal to stay down on battlefield and not advance or run to cover, a sure way to get killed, or run over by the age of disruptive outsiders, that recreate their interpretation of rules of market economy, without legacy and heritage of a tailing organization, bound by earlier commitments.

The advancements and proliferation of top-tier technology, off-the-shelf apparel; such as encrypted radio equipment, mini cameras, fake microphone pens, fabric embedded sensors, focused microphones, 'night-vision everything' are available for everyone worldwide. Anyone can arm an army of any size as needed, this is not about technological capability anymore, it is about capital. The capacity of 3D-printers is advancing rapidly, meaning that anyone can shortly build thousands of weapons, quests, bullet-proof anything, in their office backroom or in their garage. It's not only material values that are under instant change. The way individuals, companies and countries operate is more direct, instant, ruthless and faceless, with sometimes switched messages, reminding us of something familiar but sending another message, the message of altered truth. As seen in police violence across the US, authorities in general function in direct outright fashion. Today's warfare is operated remotely without the feel of a kill. Global drone operations can be controlled from Tampa, Florida making the blast of a missile in a crisis point of a foreign country. When there is an ever larger portion of wealth in society owned by a tenth of a percentage of the population, the middle-class that glues a society together, first shirts and then becomes crippled to function its part in the society, gluing both ends wealth and poor together. The miniature economies that the ultra-independence will drive are will create slews of entrepreneurs that are able to operate their online job anywhere, instead of having a nine-to-five-day-job. Individuals are better educated, knowledgeable, capable and proactively seeking to commence any practice for even a tiny advance in their well-being.

Building influence, starts with harmless looking events; cooperation of sports leagues for positive opinion, acquiring land plots beside shipping routes, tempting energy sector offers, alternative media messages, trolling, fabricated accusations, funding to ultra-leftist and rightist parties, cutting rates for favors; air force and naval presence, influencing leaders and public.

Then confusion, constant flux, fabricated stories of people and events, instability is played into societies.

The step further is to turn a partner country into a vassal, creating a pact with monologue advisory and criticism, with the final target to create a totally controlled pseudo-state, similar to Russian attempts of control over former peasants of Soviet Union. Europe's decision-making was built on flowery imagery of the late 1990's politics, thus preventing from the act of unilateral decisions, at least not quickly and determined enough, to block the reinvasion of Russian media sphere into Europe with disinformation and flux of events, mashed with a wide selection of news items, wide selection from total lies to half-truths and correct media, blended so that recipient, the viewer, is unable to clarify portions of real and unreal imagery from the broadcast. Russian intentions are to disintegrate the European Union, then slice it into pieces of influence, by supporting one country while oppressing another, and therefore set the European Union into multiple levels of confusion, with divide and conquer strategy. At the same time progressing with information flow, towards citizens in NATO countries, setting the final goal of Kremlin having the United States being unable to protect its allies, European leaders and smaller nations, and therefore ridiculing itself in front of the world.

The world is in danger of invasive media influence by opponents, both political and economic with vast media fronts of multiple content feeds, privately owned to state-controlled, everything in social media, on-demand television and broadcast TV. This does not mean a direct invasion of arms, but a constant and systematic model to approach western societies with information obfuscation, hoaxes and trickery of tailored media events to adapt and fit changing landscape of politics and market situations, with a prebuilt annual plan and calendar with flexible pre-fabricated media events.

Reference:

1. Enriques Juan, The Next species of Human
   https://www.ted.com/talks/juan_enriquez_shares_mindboggling_new_scien
   c   e?language=en

2. Alexander Dugin "Western leaders and Hollywood bubble are the enemy."

Algorithm Created Brand

Many of us have experienced the convenient ride of Uber, a popular car share service competing with the likes of Lyft, and local variants that expand rapidly around the world. Uber has been under criticism for moderating its pricing and services automatically when there is high demand for the cars, such as during natural catastrophes like floods or tornados. This may have been partly due to the new type of services being emerged and not all variants and perspectives of the operations being placed in the algorithms that control the messaging to drivers, that are independent contractors instead of traditional employers. At least that's what Uber wants to communicate to the authorities in various countries globally. As Uber's operations are controlled by fine-tuned algorithms that run the communication networks the system has based itself on, we have entered into a new era of artificial intelligence communication and media perception, that companies have begun to operate, in Uber's case, the car share service perceives for its brand and operates through its drivers (1). Uber has created itself into a powerful governing actor by ensuring its community its community management organs have been removed from the company's central offices. The company wants to distance itself from the information and disinformation that the drivers and customers create in the daily operations, but at the same time wants to control the brand, the league of drivers, publicity, brand risk and operational risks that are in the day-to-day business of carrying people of various sorts in cars around the world (2).

The company is accountable for the information flow that is taken inbound to the Uber main system; where drivers are located, how they drive, their speed, velocities resulting in driving efficiency, possible exceeding of speed limits, shifting performance and of course customer ratings, that rate not only the drivers themselves but also customers that take rides. All this data, in huge quantities, is then processed in the Uber mainframe system, with fine-tuned algorithms, that control the given rider to drivers.

At the same time, the company policies have been found sometimes limited and messaging obfuscated, creating an asymmetric information game that the central system delivers and intentionally confuses drivers. This has caused drivers to team up, comparing their rides and creating strategies beneficial to them, creating a battle, a fight between technologies that collect and analyse data and the collective human mind.

Drivers, customers and Uber central governing offices provide the public media, an ongoing volatile brand environment that need constant monitoring and control over the momentum, that has forces of the central operations and counter forces of multiple parties. All this plays into the pocket of the governing Uber by controlling the workforce, customers, but distantly, without being accountable in the eyes of government regulators and legal authorities of employee-employer governing laws. Uber's communication is tailored between partner-drivers and Uber central operations, therefore distancing the drivers from the franchise itself. This enables the company to bypass regulations of traditional employee-employer relationship. Drivers feel this refers to hypocrisy and Orwellian type of control, that has caused drivers to demand more autonomy. Drivers have installed traffic surveillance cameras to their car dashboards to produce a counter-narrative for possible customer dissatisfaction or arguments that would ruin the driver rating in the algorithm that issues them rides, and revenue, eventually causing the drivers to drive for the algorithm, instead of customers. The middleman, customer review being the key variant between an issuer of the revenue, the algorithm, and driver. Drivers have found that the rate decreases are more often a given card than an actual propeller for added sales. In driver speak, this has been phrased as "doublespeak", "propaganda" and "Orwellian total control." The more a driver takes rides, the better the Uber central system becomes in thorough knowledge, knowing when drivers are about to log off from their driving session, and the system distributes messages for the driver to keep on working, likely delivered by algorithm running the central computer system, instead of manually by a person. The system can propose drivers a fabricated demand of rides than there actually is available, similarly to rising ride prices upon sudden heavy public demand, such as a local or regional catastrophe.

In public communication Uber uses terminology such as "sharing economy" (3) expressing mutual engagement and caring proposing the consumer for a mutually assured positive outcome that benefit everyone creating a social bonding between Uber brand, its customers, drivers, but also confirmation and security towards authorities in variety of countries that the company brand operates in. The algorithm based brand management creates counter-narratives for Uber's public message; branding in the soft power environment that corporations today operate in. In Uber's case, the operations and therefore the brand, at least in part, is controlled by algorithms instead of traditional human brains. We have entered in the age of artificial intelligence of brand and publicity control (4).

References:
1. MIT Technology Review, When Your Boss Is an Uber Algorithm, December 1, 2015
2. Uber's Drivers: Information Asymmetries and Control in Dynamic Work ALEX ROSENBLAT (DATA & SOCIETY RESEARCH INSTITUTE) AND LUKE STARK (NEW YORK UNIVERSITY)1 October 15, 2015
3. Sciencedirect - Artificial intelligence and robotics in high throughput post-genomics by Aroosha Laghaee, Chris Malcolm, John Hallam, Peter Ghazal, Sep. 15, 2005
4. newsroom.uber.com/semi-automated-science-using-an-ai-simulation-framework

End Words

Events in the world increase constantly in complexity. The pace adds up the increasingly faster tempo of information creation and consumption. Every day, we have more information being created than any statesman had access to just some years back, most of the information is created during the last two years and the pace keeps exponentially climbing up. The complexities between information dimensions are getting ever more convoluted, and the relationships between matters make following some specific niche news item of a distant location nearly impossible to keep track of, without some kind of service or software to enable follow what's happening at a desired point of interest. The application economy around Twitter being a prime example of such set of tools, running in hundreds if not thousands in its assortment.

This book is written to lower the bar in understanding complex information pieces that interlink between modified news items, causes, politics, -isms, global power play and media war of leading networks, and serious attempts by hostile terrorist groups to disintegrate the civilized model of life with their *digihad* of sorts, aiming for a win by spending unlimited number of lives, compared to civilized nation-states are able to budget on arms. In our times of 'networked everything,' anyone can follow and participate at will, any cause for positive or negative, remotely, from a distance. This creates great challenges to our civilized culture, where openness and receptiveness are the mainstream trends we live in. The question is, can societies remain open to the level they would like to be, or do we have to take steps back and choose another approach to ensure safety, to prosper within our lives. A partial solution is to prevent social disintegration in our societies and promote positive values in life, instead of hate and violence oriented causes. The bogus charisma of a synthetic terroristic glamour needs to be dismantled by means of counter-persuasion and revealing the facts for masses, thereby also reaching the infected twisted terroristic messages. The media also needs to step in and implement technologies that prevent the falsified information being distributed by their state-of-the-art social networks. There needs to be room for religions of all kinds in our societies, also for Islam to progress itself into the religion of fervours, without the sword, just as modernised Catholicism of the 1970's, took over the fortress Catholicism of 1940's in the post-WWII liberation of Europe.

In America, Europe and Asia's conservatism is the stepping stone for unity and respect for minorities with equal rights a necessity, as these are essential building blocks when evolving as a modern society. Autocracy and totalitarianism are built on myths and deceit, the values and legal framework of privacy we choose for ourselves, inherit the character and volume of control. There needs to be a balance of media, freedom of speech, with an opt-out security and privacy, if there is any doubt of the administration that maintains security policies in the society, individual should have the right to opt-out. We experience the age of media manipulation for sender's benefit, creating charm, building soft power influence in the desired geographic area and its leaders. The media-war or wars-of-medias is about building influence and an immersive illusion of non-existent truths that are built-to-order, to fit and adapt to each situation of the political and event progress in our society, sometimes with instant delivery and sometimes stored to be used when appropriate for the message sender of mass persuasion.

U.S. Presidential elections amplify political celebrity narratives. The unconventional celebrity politics confuse and disrupt the conventional understanding of power. This takes persuasion towards amplification of one's message and intends to ridicule the elite in the eyes of the citizenry, to beckon the viewer to confuse one's mind. The new wave of outsiders enters politics with the likes and dislikes of masses. All this, then disseminated by broadcast media and augmented by social media, at times switching places between each other. It is essential to ensure a unified approach to the media to clarify true realities and preventing people in our nations from being distanced in our society, falling into the trap of digital –isms and the realities that exist, instead of an illusion that is systematically manufactured, refined by adversaries of our times. The age of non-consequence and no shame politics fight a balancing act with old-school big money driven power. It remains to be seen how strong the alternating trends propel our societies in 2020 and beyond.

SAMI LEINO

Appendix

Note to readers – This section applies particularly to Chapter 3.

Cold War and Popular Culture

Areas of influence in society

The United States resourced industrial scale mass persuasion in the 1980's. The same methods are operational for the benefit of Russia and China in today's world.

Influence and the related message should be adapted to focus on the group in the society that is considered the adversary, or a geographic area where influence is desired to be built at. In order to gain maximum acceptance in the percentage of the target population, the sender of the message in a mass persuasion attempt must be prepared to portray positive charm on each of the groups at all levels and areas of the society. As the messages need to be adjusted and flexible, one needs to note that there is likely a need to have competing messages for each group even though the sender of the messages is the same, usually through middlemen to obfuscate the cause and the need for influence. Below are listed some areas in society that consist of user groups, various ages, income levels, and internal influencers that act knowingly or unknowingly in favour of the cause created by the sender of propaganda.

Culture approach
Aid and art
Art exchange and cultural influence building
Language schools
Perform low bar entry-level courses for adversary language.
Trips to visit NGOs and Nonprofit organizations
Offer government subsidized trips for everyone interested.
Associations
Recreate the era of associations operating in the web.

Sports approach
Sports teams and leagues
Acquisition of hockey and soccer teams, such as the Russian KHL and the Middle East funded football (soccer) teams.

Venues and branded event halls
Acquisition of an essential and well-known arena of sports activities. Usually branded for longer periods, such as a decade, the next brand is likely to be more influential than a real business venture.

Business approach
Land grabs
Buying land spots in strategic areas to create a notion of fear and painting a vision for the press, broadcast, and telephone masts.
Business joint cooperatives
Offer and create fluently funded business with a clear upside.
Favorable deals to local business people. All transparent and legal with no change to make a loss.

Media approach
Television stations, radio stations, websites, blogs, trolls, reality television, paid articles, paid scholars articles - all of these to influence the opponent in their ways, either with direct propaganda or hidden measures with obfuscated half-truths, truths and lies. As an example, some Scandinavian radio stations broadcasted Soviet-inspired weekly episodes of fabricated radio shows that presented a fake well-being and progress of Soviet Union.

Toys and computer games
Action figures such has G.I. Joe, Cobra, Star Wars, and the like, presented Americanism at its best for younger audiences.
Missile Command, Defender, Battlezone, Centipede, and the like were computer games that put the player in the driver seat to experience the defeat of the adversary, often pointing or hinting towards Russia. Some saw the coin-op games as "breeding ground for personnel" for the defense and computer science industries, which they eventually were, at least to some degree.

TV series (some Cold war era hit series)

MacGyver (1985 - 1992) - fighting with creative high technology against rogue groups and communists depending on the theme of the episode (1980's).

The Bold and the Beautiful (since 1987) - Glamorous life in Los Angeles fashion industry.

Knight Rider (1982 - 1986) The famous car K.I.T.T with turbo boost, catching thieves and rogue adversaries with Michael Knight.

Airwolf (1984-1987) - Helicopter with superior technology.

Dallas (1978 - 1991) - Presenting prosperity and opportunity in America.

Miami Vice (1984 - 1989) Presents excitement, power, speed, and the wealth of the American lifestyle in Florida, which was the dream vacation arena of 1980's Europeans.

Love Boat (1977 - 1987) Casual entertainment presenting a desired good life in the United States for European and Scandinavian audiences in the late 1970's and 1980's.

M*A*S*H (1972 - 1983) - Presenting a surgical hospital care unit for injured service men in the Korean War of the 1950's.

Music

In 1980's Cold War era there were numerous songs to create a tempting and desired influence in the eyes of the eastern bloc citizens. Some of the most widely known are Bruce Springsteen's Born in the U.S.A, Pet Shop Boys' Go West, life is peaceful there and anti-war and anti-propaganda songs such as Another Brick in the Wall by Pink Floyd against mind control by governments, and Enola Gay, against the nuclear bombing of Hiroshima, and 19 - against the Vietnam War and war in general. In the eastern bloc, there was Alla Pugacheva with the song Million Roses, but not many others made it in the ranks of radio station hits at that time.

Motion Pictures

There are numerous other movies that present western abilities and capabilities but also the humane life, but with a fierce retaliation. Movies often create a fear - savior - hope scenario for the West's good.

The Cold War classic, Rocky IV with the showdown with Ivan Draga, the Soviet machine like appearance of actor Dolph

Lundgren against Sylvester Stallone as Rocky, resembling Rocky Marciano, an American Italian boxer from the 1950's. Eventually Rocky pushing his best and beating the humongous adversary in the final round, victimizing Rocky and creating a bully aggressor of the Russian competitor.

The Hunt for Red October - released at the end of the Cold War in 1990. Based on Tom Clancy's novel. The story is about a rogue Soviet captain who desires to defect to the United States, "Do you think they (US officials) will let me live in Montana?" asks the first officer, "I would think they'll let you live anywhere you want" responds Captain Ramius, pointing to the Soviet model of restricting location and movement of citizens.

The movie Top Gun was actually originated from the U.S. Air Force lacking fit candidates to fly the F-14 fighter, and the movie presented a glorification and glamour of U.S. fighter pilots. After the movie, which was a box office hit grossing over $356 million, recruitment figures rose to adequate levels to gain good substance for top fighter pilots programs. As a bonus, the entire western world saw the might of western air power and the entertainment factor built hegemony for a war that never was.

Firefox (movie 1982), to present adversary technology capabilities and ensure public support for a high defense budget in the United States. Based on a novel.

WarGames (1983), that plays around with the idea of supercomputers and nuclear attacks in the era of the NATO Able Archer exercise that nearly brought the world to brink of nuclear annihilation. Wargames has a strong propaganda setting, especially with the line; "Confidence is high, I repeat confidence is high," towards a Russian first strike against the U.S. and the Western world in general. There are human aspects tailored in, to have the message look humane and credible where Russia is presented as the dark, poisonous enemy and the United States as the last line of liberty on a global scale.

Red Dawn (1984), where the opening scene is about Russian paratrooper forces invading the American Heartland and how locals fight back in the quest to push out the enemy, as the movie paints a picture of Russian commercial flights coming in packed with special forces and at the same time Cuban and Nicaraguan forces fighting their way through Mexico all the way to Kansas, and Russian delivery of three armies over the Bering Strait across Alaska to join Russian troops pushing from the East Coast – eating the U.S. in one piece.

The Day After (1977 and 1983 aired on ABC network) was seen by over 100 million viewers on its initial broadcast, depicting a view of a nuclear apocalypse, presenting a strong propagandistic scenery against leadership as the main character Dr. Austin wonders, "What's going on in this world," at 32:44, and the scene of reckoning, "Do you think they are making this up," at 36:35 before an actual nuclear exchange takes place in the American Heartland in Kansas. With a U.S. retaliatory capability (38:40), "Use them or lose them... you're sitting next to the Whiteman Air Force Base... there are 150 minuteman missiles... that's an awful lot of bullseyes..."

Ice Station Zebra (1968) about a race to rescue the staff of a weather station at the North Pole. Based on an Alistair MacLean novel.

Hybrid models of the above

Mass persuasion is done as a focused and tailored campaign, Terrorist groups create additional glorification of the imagery, mash-up of video games, and movie like visuals, and romantic views of day-to-day life in the ranks of the group. Such causes may often have religious sides and added false glamour of fighting for the winning team, even though the team itself would be constantly losing, the need for men on the battlefield.

Note to readers – This section applies particularly to Chapter 6.

Message Definition of Probability

Words of estimate	Confidence	Wording
Virtually certain	99%	Almost certain (1)
Highly likely	80%	Very probable
Likely	70%	Probable
Could go either way	50%	Even
Improbable	25%	Unlikely
Doubt	10%	Very unlikely
Slight change	1%	Single digits

Reference:
1. Kent, Sherman, Words of estimate probability

Authors personal notes from a FOI Swedish Defence Research - public seminar in Helsinki, September 2015

Location: Little Parliament, Helsinki. Time: 08.00 – 10.00

- Russia uses a *Sword of Damocles* method in its principles of hard power. No try but do.
- Tactics: Do not reveal cards - no demonstrations, but only real action of hard power.
- In Russia there is *60 minute* set-up time to drive to barracks and gear up.
- Putin's regime has increased and stabilized its popularity among citizens through stated owned media.
- Opposition demonstrations are arranged and guided to suburbs out of city centers, from public view.
- Russia is *running out of spare parts* for strategic ICBM missiles.
- Russia *lags marine jet turbine knowledge* due to conflict with Ukraine.
- These capabilities will take *1-3 years* to catch up.
- Russia builds for hard power for *2020 onwards*.
- Bar to use nuclear weapons is pre-emptive and *demonstrative*. ...*MH17 style dirty bomb in Warsaw?*

Question from audience: It is claimed that United States may have capability for full or limited knock-out effect of Russian nuclear triad. Why won't U.S. use this capability if there is such? (no real answer, but rounded words from representative of defence forces).

Some of these notes have been added and amended based on FOI public news and studies. http://www.svt.se/nyheter/utrikes/russian-defence-industry-spending-doubled-in-10-years

Abusing kids in the name of God and Country

Written as a framework scheme of factual events and thoughts for this book. January 13th, 2015.

It was a clear sky Spring day of 1983, I loitered through the halls of our school in Texas, passed my red locker on the upper level, and saw a glimpse of the numbered locks my father had bought me. Janitor walked passed me and nodded "hi", I was frightened by principal's announcement. His sound was rather angry, and our teacher was actually really concerned. She asked, "Sami, what've you done?" I replied with a confused "nothing...". As I turned to left at the end of the hallway I saw secretaries in their offices looking at me with a dangerous stare, with a pitiful and somewhat disdained look. They thought I was guilty of, at least, dealing drugs, that happened in our school but I stayed away from such. Or, that I had stabbed someone with a pencil, that had also occurred between a fight with my classmate Steve and a new guy from Ciudad Juarez. As I approached the glass-walled office, the principal was there, in his 60s, bold from a top, grey, nearly white curly hair running a bit wild on the sides, fairly overweight, glasses, and usually a busy look, never a smile. He obviously tried to put on a smiley face, this time, it was something important, and gave a stiff posture, excited of importance in a weird way, but with a judging look. As I entered his office, he slid away the other door. Now I was fully and undoubtedly confused. Then, a white army man with red-brown crew-cut, older than our gym coach in her mid 30's but younger than our principal in his mid 60's entered the room. I was nearly paralyzed, who´s this guy?, I thought. My new life in the United States near the Mexican border of Ciudad Juarez, beside Biggs Air Force Base, south of White Sands Missile test area had lasted for some months, my English was rather broken on a yes and no bases so communication was limited but caught up really quick. The pudgy man said in plain Finnish but with a broken accent, "Hi Sam, how has it been, do you like it here in this school?", I replied, "It's ok, I have nice friends and our teacher is really nice.". "Well, it is nice and warm here in Texas". I agreed with a smile, nice and warm. He then said, "not cold as up north, right?". Me "Yes". It was quiet for some seconds. I looked around, what does this man want from me, maybe I could go back to my class. Then the professional in him stepped out. "Have you been to Soviet Union Sami?", "Do you speak Russian?", "Does your mother like it here?", "What does your dad do in Mexico?", "Have your parents been married for long?", "When has your mother been to Leningrad? when was it?"... It was an interrogation disguised into a nice chatter. Convenient for the opponent to answer anything. Us, myself and this army guy who happens to speak native English, pretty good Spanish, as I could make the comparison instantly to some of my friends who spoke native Spanish with their parents. His crooked Finnish accent and some Swedish combined with invasive questions into my personal things and our family made me think, "he thinks I am from the Soviet Union", "he clearly things my parents are from Leningrad." This man kept coming back, without resistance from school administrators. My both grandfathers fought the Second World War and told me stories of their war, that no one else in our relatives were interested in listening to. Everyone had heard these stories for too many times, at least for them. The details of these stories were embedded into me, I saw, what they presented, as we were skiing in the Finnish countryside. How they had thrown grenades and silenced Russian machine gun fortresses, how the machine guns do a popping sound while they are operated, it is good to duck one's head down. Mockery towards Soviets silenced uncomfortably in dinner tables. We had good chatter while cross-country skiing and watching hockey when I was after schooling at their premises and parks. I was emphasized how the war was not lost but won, as the country was independent even though 15% smaller in size and under constant threat from Soviet invasion in 1947. "Russian is a Russian, never to be trusted", "Russian stabs you in the back and cries at your grave", "Commies try to suppress entrepreneurialism, they are a threat to the society", "red-pioneers are the laughing stock, as they do not understand stocks from livestock" were the methodology that I was raised with. With that mindset, the interrogation, that I was dragged onto, in the middle of our math class felt oppressive, but from the opposite of the table. I felt uncomfortable to help out the square headed friend, as the environment was dangerous, at least that's how it felt when answering his questions. I felt tempted to cuss him in return for pressing me, how his red hair reminded me on the Soviet flag from hockey matches, but internal protection prevented to take extra steps on a mine field. The discussion between a 40ish-year-old professional counter-espionage professional and a thirteen-year-old average-in-school-rocketry-hobbyist was interesting and surely worth writing a report for one of the security agencies at the time, without question.

It was actually well played out by the military intelligence, the CIA or the FBI, as we were in a border area, this agent guy was from one of them. Before the occurrence, there had been a meet up with a German family, who were in missile training in White Sands, and my parents as all new-comers in the area met regularly. Someone that they had met informed, that they wanted to have a barbeque evening and there was a pre-set information of the notion that the friendly army guy was actually just getting to know all of us. My parents fell into the trickery right in, why wouldn't they, they had actually nothing to hide. When Soviet spies were infiltrated into the United States it was done with families similar to ours, people relocating to U.S., but not that often to a missile training area. When I told about the incident at home, there was no wondering what had happened, but rather denial, and a warning knowing my activity at school, that "that's the man that helps Germans and people like us to settle in". The German families had been warned by other families that one should not be in close encounters with us Scandinavians, as our countries return dissidents to Russia without an option to defect to West, and that they may well be spies. After all, we were right at the same spot where German scientists were given the pledge to evade Nuremberg in late 1940s' court martial, that often led to a bullet in the head or a noose around the neck conviction. Operation Paperclip operated in this very location at Fort Bliss, same Air Force Base where we lived some miles from. Dr Wernher von Braun and his best men we taken by Allied troops just before Soviets got their share of the men, with force, transported into the middle of Soviet Union. Later on, collecting stamps, I saw a photo of von Braun and President John F. Kennedy, both of them on 1960's space oriented propaganda stamps, and found difficult to understand the scene. Later this all opened my word view on the subject. After all, Wernher and his buddies were lucky, this was a place full of fast food, doughnuts, coin-ops, TV shows, Golf courses, houses with pools, families with two or more cars and the like. Abundance, a trove, of well-being at the time. In our house there was a concern of the cold war as there was in many homes, but as the missile range would have been, and still is, a primary target of intercontinental ballistic SS-20 missiles, hidden as logs in forests of Warsaw Pact countries would have been the incoming ballistic missiles, with a considerable-counter-strike-force in return, that might have saved us for another day. Whereas in Finland, as my grandfather put it, there would have been a sign "this is where Helsinki once situated". Which was worse, we will never know. It was well played out with the officials, who had taken care well ahead that no matter what I say, would be marked by the vivid imagination of a teenager. That felt wrong, but on the other hand, I know I´ve given this army fellow the rightful truth and the right answers that he wanted. No need to think, we are Russians spies to this guy as he wants to think, I though while formulating my thoughts into sentences. Our teacher wanted to know what's going on, as did my classmates. I felt our teacher knew something she didn't want to tell me, but I let it go, as I learned the language quick and went onwards to study Spanish with my Latino friends in our school. Another German guy from our class, later on, asked me, "we´re you asked a bunch of questions at principal's office?" I replied, "some, yes," but I left out it lasted for all of the math class and the science class after that, so it was at least a good afternoon discussion. He was concerned and scared, what´s going to happen to him and his family. If his background was as I understood it, likely nothing special. But he later disappeared from school without anyone knowing where he had gone to, so either our teacher played it well in tune, or she was left out of the picture. Lots of fright were shed between kids and their interrogations. Due to these instances, I decided to look the other way and become really good at baseball. "Red" was the bad guys with an intention to take our houses and cars and switch them to old Russian crappy consumer goods. While repetitive pronouncing the flag-pledge after singing the Star Spangled Banner and putting my right hand to my heart, I felt business as usual. This is how it should be, at least I rather take this than the mandatory folk dances of our very traditional school teacher in Finland.

Several months before these events, at London Heathrow immigration, a security officer pulled our relocating family off side to a separate alley for a check. Our toys, such as Matchbox die-cast little cars were thrown all over the floor. Security personnel turned upside down my brothers' box of two dozen die-cast cars. I and my brother picked up the die-cast cars as people on the security obviously intended to cause confusion, stepped on our toys and thus causing the toy vehicles with bend axles to jolt onwards. Legos threw all over, as children were clearly being to place to hit, as parents usually would have been terrified, as ours did. The security people threw everything in our suitcases around looking for filled hidden pockets. After all, we were travelling from then Soviet sphere nation state of Finland, towards missile test ground in the middle of America. Their suspicion was clear but falsely based, at a family travelling from neutral states towards the US. "You are moving to the United States, why?", "where, Texas, why?", "there is a semiconductor plant being built and..", "nope, you are on some other errands, tell us, where you come from and why?". As Finland was the developed version of a want-to-be-neutral-country at the time, it was also the optimal surroundings to transport westerly families to the United States to promote and carry out spy activities across the board. After all, the notorious man-without-a-face, Marcus Wolf, head of East German Stasi, had first been spotted at Kappelskär ferry terminal, a ferry that went to Finland and Sweden, allowing people to travel between West-ish Sweden and East-ish Finland of the time, without papers. ID free travel tradition, that changed as late as 2001, after WTC attacks.

I guess the situation at Heathrow stayed intact due to the background for being pro-western and not being totally paralysed and enraged as the security personnel intent was. This abuse, to put it at the mildest, went on throughout our journey as we were, in the counter-espionage officer eyes, "dissidents or spies", close to the Soviet border when looking from London or Texas. They looked at us, people with no harmful intentions, trying to inject the poison needle of communism to people into Texas and report of the situation regularly onwards through imagined radios. While the real spies submitted encrypted messages as they do in TV-series and movies that present those times, events knit together; by pay phones, punching in a number and a code, then attaching a men's razor like device with an encrypted hash message to the other end where it is recorded and decrypted into a clear message. Our family life was rather steady and my time in the Boy Scouts of America, exciting time to learn about night time Coyotes in the desert tent camp, and digging up a scout cottage in high mountains under masses of snow, or other similar tasks, tough traits of survival. This became a contributing balance towards Scouts of Finland, that taught me about nature on islands of the archipelago. These were the events with my approach to America, something I didn't understand right away. Watching Fall Guy and Knight Rider on evenings in 1980's, playing softball at school, practicing horseback riding on prairies and alpine skiing on the mountains of New Mexico during weekends, in the months to come, was exciting. What got my attention of the world order, as the President Ronald Reagan, Henry Kissinger, and another wise-men-of-the-time spoke in evening news broadcasts of the CBS and NBC was the news anchor, Tom Brokaw, who briefly mentioned: "Socialist country Finland had their new President elected, Mr. Koivisto..." socialist country?... But, we're not a socialist country! Finland was under the influence of a foreign power, Soviet Union, so this was what my grandfather had advised me of, "never let your vigilance drop."

Little did I know, that it was my first touch to Cold War.

Sources

University of Turku – American Study Group lectures January-March, 2015. History, economics, finance, intelligence, media, motion imagery, trauma of an image, defense, popular media, socio-demographic structures and culture of America, Canada and Mexico – and the international relations and ramifications.

Author's living, studies, observances and working in United States, 1981-1983, 1997, 2011-2012.

A
Artificial intelligence and robotics in high throughput post-genomics - Sciencedirect - by Aroosha Laghaee, Chris Malcolm, John Hallam, Peter Ghazal, Sep. 15, 2005

B
Berger Heidi, Venäjän Informaatio-psykologinen sodankäyntitapa (in Finnish), 2010.
Blumn William, Rogue State: A Guide to the World's Only Superpower, 2015, Common Courage Press

C
Chomsky Noam, Mc Chesney Robert W. Profit over People, 2011
China's Charm: Implications of Chinese Soft Power, June 2006
China's great game: Road to a new empire, Financial Times, Oct. 12.
The China Journal, Chigaco Journals, January 2007.
China's Propaganda System: Institutions, Processes and Efficacy by David Shambaugh, The China Journal No. 57, Jan. 2007. Pp. 25-58 by Chicago Journals
China's Military Strategy, source: Xinhua 2015-05-26
China's Real Blue Water Navy, Andrew Erickson, August 30, 2012
Choking the Social Networks Revolution, Belarus Digest 25th July 2011.
The Clandestine Cold War in Asia, 1945-65: Western Intelligence, Propaganda and Special Operations, Richard J Aldrich, Ming-Yeh Rawnsley, 2000.
Carnegie Endownment, China's Charm: Implications of Chinese Soft Power, June 2006
The CMO's Guide to Programmatic Buying by Tim Peterson, Alex Kantrowitz, AD AGE, published on May 19, 2014.
Cooperative and continuous foresight – A Proposal for national foresight approach, Prime Ministers Office Reports, 2/2014
The Cultural Sociology of Political Assassination: Ron Eyerman

D
The Diplomat, June 5th, 2015.
Adapted from Discussion of Richards J. Heur, Jr., personal communication with Gordon Mitchell, 9. July 2005.
Doroshevich Mikhail, Users of social media in Belarus

E
Earnhardt, Rebecca L. Al-Qaeda's media strategy, Internet self-radicalization and counter-radicalization policies, Virginia Commonwealth University, approx. 2013.
The Economist May 23rd 2015, Aug 23rd 2007, August 29th 2015, September 5th 2015, May 30th 2015, June 13th 2015, January 2016.

F
FIIA China Research Days 2015 "Awakening to China's Dream – Domestic realities, global ramifications"
FIIA Media Power in International Politics, Sept. 10, 2015
FIIA Magazine Ulkopolitiikka 1/2015. P. 44-58 (in Finnish).

FIIA No More Marching: The Kremlin suppresses nationalist movements in order to achieve a like-minded society – November 2015.
FIIA No Change on the Horizon, Belarus 2015 Presidential Election, Arkady Moshes & Andras Racz, September 2015
FIIA Obama's Foreign Policy Fiia Briefing Paper - October 2015
FIIA Power Transformation, Sept. 9 2015, Helsinki
FIIA Topicality of Separation of Powers – The US Congress and Foreign Policy Processes – August 2015
FIIA Russian Protest On and Offline Briefing Paper February 2012
FIIA Analysis, December 2015, Zugzwang in slow motion?
FIIA.fi Crafting The EU Global Strategy, December 2015
FIIA.fi Media Power in International Politics, September 10, 2015
FIIA.fi Putin's Reactive Reforms, December 2013
Financial Times, multiple editions, 2015.

G
Gough Susan L. Ltc. The Evolution of Strategic Influence, United States Army.
Genrdon Angela, Al Qaida: Propaganda and Media Strategy, Integrated Threat Assesment Center, 2007

H
Heinonen Yrjö (toim.), Taide, kokemus ja maailma - Risteyksiä tieteidenväliseen taiteidentutkimukseen
(in Finnish), Utukirjat 2014 p. 22, 24-26, 29, 57.
Holt Douglas, Harward Business Review, March 2016
Hytönen Kaisa, Suomen maabrändäyksen taustasyyt ja toimintamallin kehittäminen, 2012, Lapin Yliopistopaino (in Finnish).

I
Iloniemi Jaakko, Vallan Käytävillä, 1999.
ISIS; The Explosion of Narratives – The Land of the Revolution Between Political and Metaphysical Eternities http://jadaliyya.com

J
Järvinen Petteri, NSA - Näin Meitä Seurataan, 2014, p. 38-40.

K
Kanava Suomalainen Suomi 06/2015.
Keller William W. Preventive Force: Untangling the Discourse.
Graduate School of Public and International Affairs and Gordon R. Mitchell, Department of Communications - 2006, University of Pittsburgh
Kent Sherman, Words of estimate probability.
Kissinger Henry, World Order, 2014.

L
Left Catholicism 1943-1955: Catholics and Society in Western Europe at the Point of Liberation
Leibowitz Mark, New York Times, Feb. 17. 2016.
Leino, Sami, Startup Africa (Chapter: Terrorism)
Lynch Marc, Al-Qaeda's Media Strategies, The National Interest, Spring 2006
Lewis, Karlanna, When Rap Music is a Crime, The Atlantic, March 7th, 2015.

M
Maarten Albarda personal blog, Man vs. machine, the advent of electronic buying and the death of the media buyer, Monday, September 16, 2013.
Madson Pter M. Perils and Profits: A Reexamination of the Link Between Profitability and Safety in U.S. Aviation, Bringham Young University, 3rd March 2013
Media Control, Second Edition: The Spectacular Achievements of Propaganda by Noam Chomsky.
Media principles: Killed by friendly fire in US infowar, Index On Censorship (2002).
Mann Michael, Incoherent Empire, 2003

N

Naim, Moses, The End of Power, 2014
Nye Joseph S. Jr. Is the American Century Over, 2014
New York Times 2015/12/13

O

Oskoei M.A, Artificial Intelligence, 22/09/2014, http://cs.insightglobe.com

P

Patil Roman, Why automated media buying is the future of mobile app advertising, The Economic Times, 29 Sep, 2015.
Popovic Srdja, Adaptation from A Guide To Effective Nonviolent Struggle, students book, 2007 Beograd: DMD. Powers of pillar and methods and techniques.
Post-Soviet Russian identity and its influence on European-Russian relations, March 20th 2015.

R

Rotman David, MIT Technology Review, Who will own the robots? June 15, 2015.
Ruotsista tuli automaattisodan liipasin, Magazine Rauhanpuollustajat 6/2014
Russia: 7-year cyberwar against Nato, EU and US by Kremlin-sponsored hackers – The Dukes exposed, September 17, 2015

S

Simons Greg, Mass Media and Modern Warfare - p. 53-55, 60 - 65, 89-93
Sternberg, Robert J, The Nature of Hate.
Screenmediadaily.com
Singularity Hub – These Technologies Will Shift the Global Balance of Power in the Next 20 Years, Oct 6, 2015
Soft Power by Joseph S. Nye Jr. 2014
Strategisen painopisteen siirtymät ja suurstrategian suuntaviivat (in Finnish), Kosmopolis – Vol 45: 2/2015
Successful Crisis Management in the Airline Industry, Barcelor Thesis: Anna Hansson, Tomas Vikström, 2011-01-05, Uppsala University
Switching to digital: Presidential elections in Belarus blogs.fco.gov.uk
State Council Information Office Issues "China's Military Strategy", Xinhua, 2015 May 26th.
Sullivan Alexander, Erikcson Andrew S. Big Story Behind China's New Military Strategy, June 05, 2015

T

Teaching with Document Series, National Archives, by Jo Anne Gill 1993.
Themes of Soviet Strategic Deception and Disinformation by John Lenczowski - 1987
The Ten Commandments of Propaganda by Brian Anse Patrick 2011.
To win, to lose, to boycott: Belarusian presidential run 2015
Tämä oli Neuvostoliitto (in Finnish), 28/09/2015, Helsingin Sanomat
Tupi Marian, German Chelsea, Human Progress, 2016-02-17

U

Uber's Drivers: Information Asymmetries and Control in Dynamic Work
ALEX ROSENBLAT (DATA & SOCIETY RESEARCH INSTITUTE) AND LUKE STARK (NEW YORK UNIVERSITY)1 October 15, 2015
Ulkopolitiikka magazines (in Finnish), 2014, 2015
United Nations Human Rights - Belarus Elections - Neither Free Nor Fair
U.S. Spy Chief: Get Ready for Everything to be hacked All of the Time, Foreign Policy 09/2015

V

Vehkoo, Johanna, Yle.fi: Valheenpalajastaja: Sosiaalinen Media Sumentaa Kritiikin, Feb. 15, 2016. 2.

W

Wilcox Laird, Propaganda, Persuasion and Deception, Over 1.120 selected quotations for the ideological scaptic, 2005

What ISIS Really Wants? The Atlantic 03/2015.
Wikipedia: Pussy Riot, Missile Command arcade game, Grand Theft Auto video game.
When Your Boss Is an Uber Algorithm, MIT Technology Review, December 1, 2015.

Web and Reports

The Families Funding Presidential Election
http://www.nytimes.com/interactive/2015/10/11/us/politics/2016-presidential-election-super-pac-donors.html
Google Connected to brain http://www.ibtimes.co.uk/ray-kurzweil-human-brains-could-be-connected-cloud-by-2030-1504403
MH17, KAL007 http://journal-neo.org/2014/07/21/kal-007-case-shows-parallels-with-malaysian-airlines-mh17/ and the Time, September 13, 1983 in the article, author's interpretation of 1983's personal view of media projectile.
Laffer Curve – Wikipedia https://en.wikipedia.org/wiki/Laffer_curve
Iran Hostage Crisis https://en.wikipedia.org/wiki/Iran_hostage_crisis
Pierce R. Justin, Schott K. Peter, THE SURPRISINGLY SWIFT DECLINE OF U.S. MANUFACTURING EMPLOYMENT, NATIONAL BUREAU OF ECONOMIC RESEARCH, 2012
https://www.usitc.gov/research_and_analysis/documents/Pierce%20and%20Schott%20%20The%20Surprisingly%20Swift%20Decline%20of%20U.S.%20Manufacturing%20Employment_0.pdf
Enriques Juan, The Next species of Human
https://www.ted.com/talks/juan_enriquez_shares_mindboggling_new_science?language=en
https://cchs.gwu.edu/sites/cchs.gwu.edu/files/downloads/Berger_Occasional%20Paper.pdf
http://malbarda.blogspot.fi/2013/09/man-vs-machine-advent-of-electronic.html
http://newsroom.uber.com/semi-automated-science-using-an-ai-simulation-framework
http://www.theatlantic.com/video/archive/2012/09/60-years-of-presidential-attack-ads-in-one-video/262115/
https://quizlet.com/5435505/7-types-of-propaganda-techniques-flash-cards/
http://presidential-power.com/?p=3936
http://www.overalltech.net/pub/Quotations-Propaganda.pdf
http://www.globalissues.org/article/157/war-propaganda-and-the-media
http://www.globalissues.org/article/399/killed-by-friendly-fire-in-us-infowar
http://www.globalissues.org/issue/245/war-on-terror
http://www.globalissues.org/article/352/mainstream-media-and-propaganda
http:// handle.dtic.mil/100.2/ADA403848
http://ctb.ku.edu/en/table-of-contents/advocacy/respond-to-
http://counterattacks/overview-of-opposition-tactics/main
singularityhub.com/2015/10/06, Singularity Hub, These Technologies will shift the global balance of power in the next 20 years
https://en.wikipedia.org/wiki/Nayirah_(testimony)
http://nytimes.com/2015/12/08
http://bbc.com
http://cnn.com
http://hs.fi
http://uusisuomi.fi
http://livingroomcandidate.org
The Atlantic.com 2014 - 2015.
Allianz IoT World, Nov. 19, 2015.
KPMG, Business in the Hyper-Connected World.
RedHat Report, DRIVING DIGITAL TRANSFORMATION: NEW SKILLS FOR LEADERS, NEW ROLE FOR THE CIO, May 2015.
https://hbr.org/resources/pdfs/comm/RedHat/RedHatReportMay2015.pdf

http://www.svt.se/nyheter/utrikes/russian-defence-industry-spending-doubled-in-10-years
Russell Raynold's Digital Transformational Leaders, 2015
Wikipedia: Transformational Leadership
World Economic Forum - Risk Responsibility Hyperconnected World Report 2014

Broadcast and Streaming Television, Music

TV-Series Madam Secretary, State of Affairs, Homeland, Little Mosque on the Prairie, Knight Rider, McGyver, Wargames, First Strike, Rocky, Rambo, Top Gun, All in the Family, Red Dawn, The Day After, Ice station Zebra, Firefox, Hunt of the Red October.
Bruce Springsteen, Pet Shop Boys, Pink Floyd, Alla Pugacheva.
Fox News, 2001, 2014, 2015
CNBC, September 11, 2001
RT, October - November 2015
YLE, January – December 2015
Youtube.com – Vice News
Youtube.com – Sortiment of motion picture and audio of 1970's, 1980's, 1990's

Recordings and Podcasts

Lecturers of UTU, FIIA and FOI
YLE Areena – Jari Sarasvuo, January 2016
Speeches from Paasikivi Seura – Former Prime Minister of Finland, Matti Vanhanen.

SAMI LEINO

Reports of my death have been greatly exaggerated.

-Marc Twain-

Made in the USA
San Bernardino, CA
24 February 2018